the amazing make-ahead
baby food book

the amazing make-ahead baby food book

Make Three Months of Homemade Purees in Three Hours

LISA BARRANGOU, PhD

Photography by Erin Scott

TEN SPEED PRESS
Berkeley

Published in the United States by Ten Speed Press, an imprint of the Crown Publishing Group, a division of Random House LLC, a Penguin Random House Company, New York.
www.crownpublishing.com
www.tenspeed.com

Ten Speed Press and the Ten Speed Press colophon are registered trademarks of Random House LLC.

Originally published in slightly different form as *RealSmart Baby Food* by RealFood Doctor Press in 2013.

Library of Congress Cataloging-in-Publication Data

Barrangou, Lisa
[Realsmart baby food]
The amazing make-ahead baby food book : make 3 months of homemade purees in 3 hours / Lisa Barrangou, PhD. — First ten speed press edition.
     pages cm
Previously published under title: *Realsmart baby food*.
Includes bibliographical references and index.
1. Baby foods. 2. Make-ahead cooking. 3. Infants—Nutrition. 4. Cooking (Soft foods) I. Title.
RJ216.B273 2015
641.3'00832—dc23

2014023149

Hardcover ISBN: 978-1-60774-714-7
eBook ISBN: 978-1-60774-715-4

Printed in China

Design by Margaux Keres

10 9 8 7 6 5 4 3

First Ten Speed Press Edition

For my three babies, Benjamin, Emilie, and Patrick, who inspired the content of this book, and everything else that I do. May you find your passion, learn to live it, and be the change.

PREFACE

As a food professional who has previously worked for three different Fortune 500 food companies as a food scientist, I have seen firsthand what processed food truly is. What it is *not* is fresh, naturally nutrient-rich, naturally beautiful, flavorful, real food. When I had my first child, I immediately knew that homemade baby food—made from whole, real foods, with no additives or fillers—would be my baby's food source. In 2005, I exited the corporate food world, and my homemade baby food—making journey began.

By the time I had my third child, I had developed quite an efficient system for making baby food. Several of my mommy friends were impressed with my ability to provide homemade baby food for so long, never giving up to rely on processed jarred foods. I had many friends who had attempted to make baby food themselves, but the biggest challenge was always figuring out how to provide a diverse assortment of foods. They would invariably give up at some point and resort to processed jarred foods because they just could not figure out how to offer enough variety without spending countless hours in the kitchen making purees. Every once in a while, I would make extra-large batches of purees to share with these mommy friends, and they were always so appreciative of the variety that I brought. Realizing that I was adding real value to the baby food eating experience, I eventually started a homemade baby food business called the Green Baby Chef.

I optimized my efficient system to be able to create three months' worth of wholesome, delicious baby food in three hours. I would shop for and bring fresh whole foods into a client's home, create three months' worth of baby food in their kitchen, and leave the food compactly stored in their freezer, along with a suggested meal plan. While many parents appreciated my service, many other parents, who were impressed and inspired, wanted to implement my system themselves. I have been asked countless times to share tips and recipes, and the details of my "three months in three hours" strategy. This book does just that.

I have developed a wonderfully efficient, flexible, comprehensive homemade baby food plan for you to implement at home. This plan includes every detail you need to create a well-balanced, diverse selection of whole food purees and freshly ground grains to feed your baby for up to three months, and to do it within three one-hour blocks of time. Rather than providing you with elaborate recipes, *The Amazing Make-Ahead Baby Food Book* guides you to prepare whole foods individually, using single-ingredient recipes, and then shows you how to combine your individual creations for an endless number of flavorful, nutritionally balanced meal possibilities. In addition to recipes, this comprehensive plan includes detailed sourcing guidelines, shopping lists, guidelines for how to use each one-hour block of time, a three-month sample menu, in-depth nutritional information, and much more. The plan is flexible enough to take you through the various stages of your baby's palate development, and the information prepares you for knowing how to feed your baby wholesome foods for a lifetime.

I hope this book will help you feed your baby only the best that nature provides in an amazingly efficient amount of time. The recipes in this book are for foods that my babies started out eating—the same foods they eat today. The only difference is I do not have to puree them anymore. I firmly believe that if you start babies off with flavorful whole foods, they will know what real food is, and they will desire it as they grow.

From one parent to another, *bon appétit*!

INTRODUCTION

Creating a well-balanced, diverse offering of meals that baby will enjoy can be the most challenging part of feeding your baby. This challenge is largely responsible for why so many parents leave it up to food companies to create and supply their baby's food for them. While commercially processed jarred baby food does offer convenience, homemade baby food made from fresh whole foods is far superior, both in nutrient and flavor quality.

Whole foods are foods that are unprocessed and unrefined (or processed and refined as little as possible), and therefore maintain their natural flavor and nutrient integrity. Think of whole foods as those that can typically be found in nature, like whole fruits, vegetables, unrefined grains, and fresh cuts of meat. Processed jarred and pouched baby foods, while made mostly, but not entirely, from whole foods, are subject to very high temperature and pressure treatments, which allow them to remain shelf stable for literally years but result in substantial nutrient and flavor loss. The impact of this high heat can be clearly seen by comparing the color of processed jarred pea puree with homemade pea puree. The dramatic color change that results from excess heat directly indicates nutrient and flavor quality loss. In addition to extensive processing, jarred baby foods often include thickening agents, such as flours, starches, and gums, to increase stability (prevent them from separating during long-term storage), effectively diluting the nutrient density of the product.

Homemade baby food, on the other hand, can be prepared using gentle cooking methods, ensuring the maximum retention of nutrient and flavor integrity. Storing homemade baby food in the freezer is a gentle preservation method that locks in nutrients rather than destroying them, allowing this nutrient and flavor integrity to carry over until consumption. When babies are offered gently processed, flavorful whole food purees, they learn to accept and enjoy the natural, beautiful flavors that nature provides. This early acceptance, if cultivated, becomes a preference, and carries on with babies through life. Conversely, the bland flavors of jarred baby food purees often lead to an underdeveloped palate that is less accepting of the full flavors of healthy foods, and that, too, can be carried on through life.

Making homemade baby food provides an opportunity for you to prepare whole foods for your baby right from the start. Researchers have found that consumption patterns for fruits and vegetables often change adversely as babies transition from purees to a mature diet, primarily due to the introduction of processed foods. One study researched food consumption patterns of US infants and toddlers and found that, while deep yellow vegetables were consumed by 39 percent of babies at seven to eight months old, that percentage sharply declined to 13 percent at nineteen to twenty-four months old, when french fries became the most commonly consumed vegetable. This study also found that at nineteen to twenty-four months old, nearly one-third of babies consumed no fruit, while 60 percent consumed baked desserts, 20 percent consumed candy, and 44 percent consumed sweetened beverages on a given day.[1] In our current Western food culture, many well-intentioned parents unwittingly fall into the processed food trap. And no matter how healthily you may have eaten before you had children, it can be even harder to find the time for fresh-food preparation once they come along. I hope this simple system will make it easier for you to quickly and confidently keep whole foods at the forefront of your child's eating habits—even as life becomes increasingly more complex.

Preparing homemade baby food is very easy to do, but it does take time, the right cooking tools, and planning to provide a diverse, well-balanced offering of age-appropriate food. *The Amazing Make-Ahead Baby Food Book* does most of the planning for you, guiding you through a six-step process that will prepare you to make three months' worth of baby food in just three one-hour blocks of time. After guiding you through preparing a large supply of individual whole food purees, this book shows you how to combine your individual purees into an endless variation of flavorful, nutritionally balanced meals, and then transitions you to preparing more advanced meals as your baby approaches readiness for a mature diet.

As you begin your baby food making adventure be sure to read chapter 2, which provides valuable information on feeding timelines, specific health concerns to be aware of, safe food preparation practices, and selection and preparation tips for whole foods. Please note that this book has been written as an informative guide to support your baby's health and nutrition, but it is not intended as a substitute for the medical advice of a physician. Always consult your baby's pediatrician for health-related matters or concerns. Now, let's get started!

1. Fox, M. K., S. Pac, B. Devaney, and L. Jankowski. "Feeding Infants and Toddlers Study: What Foods Are Infants and Toddlers Eating?" *Journal of the American Dietetic Association* 104, no. 1, supplement 1 (2004): S22–S30.

CHAPTER 1

the amazing make-ahead strategy

••

The Amazing Make-Ahead Strategy will guide you through six steps to create three months' worth of wholesome, delicious, nutritious baby food in three one-hour blocks of time:

1. SELECT A MENU OF WHOLE FOODS
2. PREPARE A SHOPPING LIST
3. CREATE SPACE
4. SHOP FOR WHOLE FOODS
5. CREATE A *MISE EN PLACE* PLAN
6. PREPARE BABY FOOD

Steps 1 through 5 will prepare you for your three cooking sessions (step 6). Each cooking session will be spent preparing one-third of the baby food. These three different sessions, each separated by at least one day, minimize equipment needs and freezer space during the initial freezing process. Afterward, you will have three months' worth of baby food made and compactly stored, and you will be ready to start feeding your baby. With this chapter's three-month menu of meals, plus the handy Flavor Compatibility Guide and tips on mix-ins, building amazing meals is a snap.

The Six Steps

The Amazing Make-Ahead Strategy is a flexible plan that allows you to build a custom baby food supply using whole foods of your choice. You also have the option to use the sample menu, shopping list, and *mise en place* plan provided in this book, instead of creating your own. This strategy will show you how to turn the ingredients you see on the opposite page into the compact basket of cubes pictured on page 23.

Step 1: Select a Menu of Whole Foods

The first step of the Amazing Make-Ahead Strategy is to choose the whole foods you would like to use to create your three-month supply of baby food. Refer to Simple Puree Recipes in chapter 3 to choose a total of eighteen different fruits, vegetables, and legumes to puree, plus two or three whole grains to grind, taking care to choose foods that encompass a rainbow of colors. I recommend the following quantities of whole food categories to allow optimal flexibility for creating flavorful, nutritionally balanced meals: 8–9 fruits, 6–7 vegetables, and 3–4 legumes (for a total of 18), plus 2–3 whole grains. *Note*: you can also make lentil and split pea flours in addition to the 18 whole foods, as these legumes are "dry-grind" recipes and therefore do not require use of the freezer trays for preparation.

If building your own menu from scratch, refer to the Flavor Compatibility Guide later in this chapter when making whole food selections, as you will gradually begin combining these individual whole foods into balanced meals. Otherwise, use the Amazing Whole Foods Menu provided below, which is designed to make the food-planning process easier while offering a robust variety of flavor and nutrients.

The Amazing Whole Foods Menu will produce a rainbow of approximately 270 frozen fruit, vegetable, and legume puree cubes, plus whole grain and legume cereals.

AMAZING WHOLE FOODS MENU

FRUITS
Apples •• Avocados •• Bananas
Blueberries •• Cherries •• Mangoes
Peaches •• Pears •• Prunes

VEGETABLES
Broccoli •• Butternut squash •• Carrots
Kale •• Parsnips •• Sweet potatoes

LEGUMES
Black beans •• Haricots verts
Red lentils •• Sweet peas

GRAINS
Brown rice •• Oats •• Quinoa

AMAZING WHOLE FOODS SHOPPING LIST

WHOLE FOOD	AMOUNT	SELECTION TIPS	AVAILABLE FROZEN*	DIRTY DOZEN**	CLEAN 15**	
Apples	1½ pounds (or 5 medium)	Avoid tart varieties. Choose: Golden/Red Delicious, Gala, Fuji, Jonagold, Braeburn; firm with no bruising		🍎		FRUITS
Avocados	1½ pounds (or 4 medium)	Gently squeeze for slight softness; tight skin, no spotting, no aroma			◎	FRUITS
Bananas	1½ pounds (or 5 medium)	Cavendish, yellow, not a lot of brown or green				FRUITS
Blueberries	1 pint (or 16 ounces)	Firm, dry, plump, smooth skins, white bloom, no mold	❄			FRUITS
Cherries	1 pound	Taste for sweetness; firm with no wrinkles	❄			FRUITS
Mangoes	1½ pounds (or 3 large)	Smell at stem end for mango aroma; should yield to gentle pressure	❄		◎	FRUITS
Peaches	1½ pounds	Soft, not too firm, peach aroma, no green color	❄	🍎		FRUITS
Pears	1½ pounds (or 5 medium)	Bartlett, Anjou, Bosc, Comice, Asian; smell and apply pressure just below stem for slight softness				FRUITS
Prunes	⅓ pound (or 15 individual)	No additives (sulfites, sugar); already pitted				FRUITS
Broccoli	1 pound florets	Firm, compact florets, dark green, no brown or yellow	❄			VEGETABLES
Butternut squash	1¼ pounds	Intact stem, dull-colored skin, no shiny skin or bruising	❄			VEGETABLES
Carrots	1¼ pounds	Thin, smooth shape, bright color, greens not wilted; not soft or rubbery				VEGETABLES
Kale	1½ pounds with ribs, or 1 pound loose leaf	Deep green, no yellow, brown, or wilting; small-medium leaves	❄	🍎		VEGETABLES
Parsnips	1¼ pounds	Choose smallest, whitest				VEGETABLES
Sweet potatoes	1¼ pounds	Garnet, Jewel, Beauregard; firm, no decay			◎	VEGETABLES
Black beans	2 (15-ounce) cans	No salt; BPA-free liner (such as Eden Organic brand)				LEGUMES
Haricots verts	1 pound	Bright green, crisp, thin, not too stiff	❄			LEGUMES
Red Lentils	1 cup (or ½ pound)	Dry, firm, clean, unwrinkled, uniform color				LEGUMES
Sweet peas	2 pounds fresh pods or 1 pound shelled	Pods: small, firm, green with no yellow or wilting; Peas: bright green, small, firm. Taste for sweetness	❄		◎	LEGUMES
Brown rice	1 cup (or ½ pound)	Check use-by date; smell bulk container				GRAINS
Oats	1 cup (or ½ pound)	Certified gluten free; any form; check use-by date; smell bulk container				GRAINS
Quinoa	1 cup (or ½ pound)	Prerinsed (such as Bob's Red Mill brand)				GRAINS

* If selecting frozen, purchase one 16-ounce (1-pound) bag.

** The Environmental Working Group (EWG) recommends purchasing organic versions of produce on the Dirty Dozen Plus list, while indicating organic may not be necessary for produce on the Clean 15 list (see page 52).

You could also use the Amazing Whole Foods Menu as a template, and substitute any whole food as desired (for example, substitute spinach for kale, pumpkin for butternut squash, and so on). The shopping list, *mise en place* plan, and three-month menu of meals provided in this chapter are all built from this Amazing Whole Foods Menu.

Step 2: Prepare a Shopping List

After selecting your menu, prepare your shopping list. See the sample shopping list the opposite page. To create your own shopping list, refer to Simple Puree Recipes in chapter 3 for quantities and other details of whole foods needed. Your list can include an indication of which foods may be found frozen if unavailable fresh, notes on how to select produce, whether or not organic is necessary, substitutions you will use if some foods are not available, and so on. Here is a key to the icons used throughout this book:

AVAILABLE FROZEN ❄
This food is typically available frozen (see page 51).

CLEAN 15 ☺
This food is part of the Clean 15 list (see page 52).

DIRTY DOZEN PLUS 🍎
This food is part of the Dirty Dozen Plus list (see page 52)

EDIBLE SKINS FOR LATER ⵣ
This food has skins that should be peeled before ten to twelve months of age (see page 55).

Step 3: Create Space

After the shopping list has been developed, create space for storing the whole foods you plan to bring home. Have adequate refrigerator, freezer, and counter storage space available.

Once the whole foods have been pureed, sufficient freezer space to store six freezer trays after each cooking session is necessary. The stackable silicone freezer trays used in this book (see page 11) each measure 4½ inches wide by 7¼ inches deep by 1¼ inches tall. Once frozen, puree cubes will be transferred from their freezer trays to labeled freezer storage bags, which should then be organized in a freezer storage basket for easy handling. The freezer storage basket used in this book to hold a three-month supply of baby food measures 11¾ inches wide by 12½ inches deep by 7½ inches tall (see page 23).

Step 4: Shop for Whole Foods

Bring the shopping list created in step 2 and head out to do your shopping! Bring your whole foods home and store appropriately until ready for preparation. Refer to chapter 2 for tips on selection, storage, and controlling ripening.

Step 5: Create a Mise en Place Plan

After all whole foods have been procured, make an organized plan for preparing them. *Mise en place* (pronounced "meez ahn plahs") is a French term that literally means "put into place." This phrase is used among food professionals to refer to getting "everything in place" before beginning food preparation. A *mise en place* plan details what equipment, tools, and ingredients are going to be used, what is going to be done, and in what order, allowing the chef to work efficiently. A *mise en place* plan will help avoid last-minute trips to the grocery or kitchenware store because something was forgotten. Prepare the plan after you do your shopping, just in case last-minute food substitutions have to be made. Use the *mise en place* plan provided on the following pages, or use the following tips to develop a *mise en place* plan tailored to your specific menu, incorporating details from your chosen simple puree recipes in chapter 3.

- Divide individual foods equally among the three cooking sessions by evenly spreading out "no-cook" recipes (which take the least amount of time) and recipes with longer cook times (like winter squash or root vegetables), to keep each session balanced at approximately one hour long. Each session should use six whole food recipes requiring freezer trays (all recipes except "dry-grind" recipes require freezer trays).

- Make sure all necessary equipment and cooking tools are written into the *mise en place* plan.

- Thaw any frozen "no-cook" foods by the time the cooking session begins. (Frozen foods that will be cooked do not need to be thawed beforehand.)

- Avoid being idle by planning to prepare "no-cook" recipes and do other tasks while foods cook.

- Plan to "dry-grind" grains, lentils, and split peas at the beginning of a cooking session, to ensure availability of a dry blender/food processor bowl.

- Foods that take the longest time to cook should be started first.

Step 6: Prepare Baby Food

Now you are ready to make baby food! Start each cooking session with your specific *mise en place* plan and individual whole food recipes available for referencing. Read the *mise en place* plan and recipes from start to finish, then implement the plan, laying out all equipment and ingredients before beginning. In each cooking session, you will prepare six whole food purees and "dry-grind" one

or more whole foods. Note that a quick rinse of the blender is all that is necessary between purees.

When the first cooking session is finished, freeze the purees for at least 24 hours (or until completely solid). The second and third cooking sessions can start any time after the frozen puree cubes have been transferred into freezer storage bags, at which time the freezer trays will be available for use again. By the end of session 3, you will have three months' worth of baby food made, compactly stored, and ready for feeding baby!

TOOLS NEEDED

A few basic tools are needed for preparing and storing homemade baby food. These tools are not baby-food specific, so they can be used well into the future. For a detailed discussion of these tools, see Appendix B, page 174.

Blender/food processor

Cherry pitter (optional)

Colander

Cutting board

Freezer storage bags, 1-quart (18)

Freezer storage basket

Freezer trays, silicone, 15 (1-ounce) cube capacity (6)

Gloves (one pair insulating, three pairs disposable)

Knife

Plastic wrap or waxed paper

Pot (small) with lid

Prep bowls (6)

Rubber spatula

Steamer

Storage containers with lids (8)

Timer

Trash bowl

Vegetable peeler

COOKING SESSION 1 •• AMAZING MISE EN PLACE PLAN

			START		10 MIN
no-cook	BANANAS		peel		puree & pour
	BLUEBERRIES	wash			
		HEAT WATER IN A STEAMER TO A SIMMER			
steam	APPLES	wash	peel	cut	
	CARROTS	wash	peel	cut	steam 8-10 min.
	HARICOTS VERTS	wash		cut	
	SWEET PEAS	wash			
dry-grind	BROWN RICE				grind

before you begin

lable freezer storage bags

shell sweet peas (if using fresh)

thaw frozen "no-cook" foods

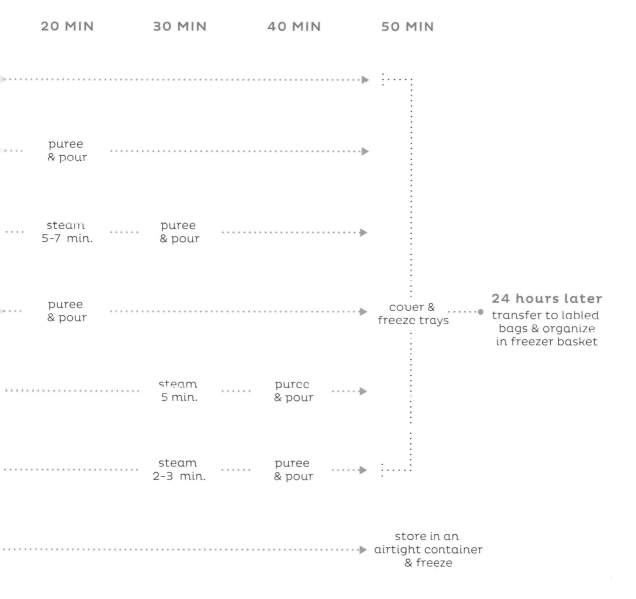

20 MIN   30 MIN   40 MIN   50 MIN

puree
& pour

steam   puree
5-7 min.   & pour

puree   cover &   24 hours later
& pour   freeze trays   transfer to labled
                                                                bags & organize
                                                                in freezer basket

                steam   puree
                5 min.   & pour

                steam   puree
                2-3 min.   & pour

                                                store in an
                                                airtight container
                                                & freeze

COOKING SESSION 2 •• AMAZING MISE EN PLACE PLAN

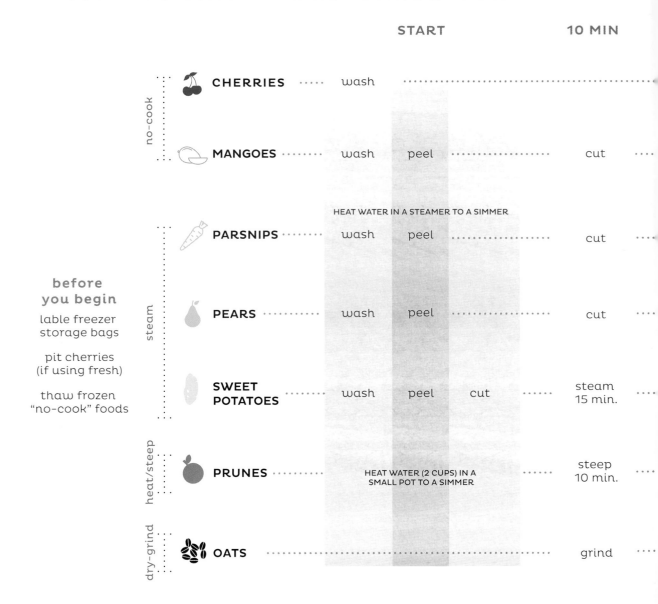

			START		10 MIN
no-cook	🍒 **CHERRIES**	wash			
	🥭 **MANGOES**	wash	peel		cut
steam			HEAT WATER IN A STEAMER TO A SIMMER		
	🥕 **PARSNIPS**	wash	peel		cut
	🍐 **PEARS**	wash	peel		cut
	🍠 **SWEET POTATOES**	wash	peel	cut	steam 15 min.
heat/steep	🍑 **PRUNES**	HEAT WATER (2 CUPS) IN A SMALL POT TO A SIMMER			steep 10 min.
dry-grind	🌰 **OATS**				grind

before you begin

lable freezer storage bags

pit cherries (if using fresh)

thaw frozen "no-cook" foods

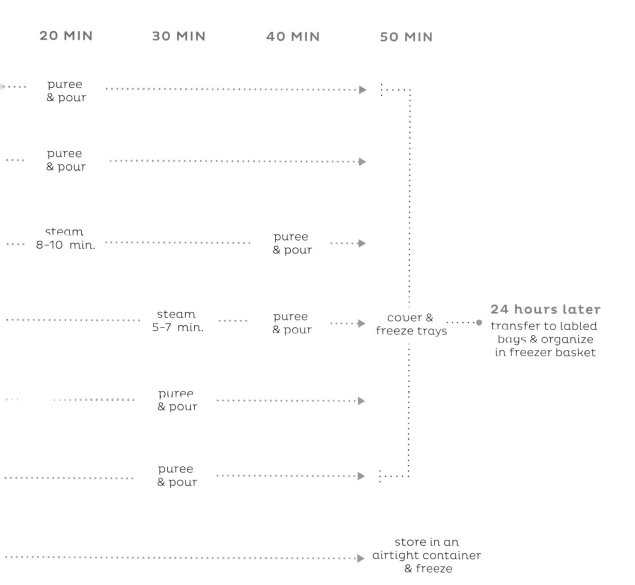

20 MIN   30 MIN   40 MIN   50 MIN

puree
& pour

puree
& pour

steam
8-10 min.   puree
                            & pour

            steam   puree   cover &   **24 hours later**
            5-7 min.   & pour   freeze trays   transfer to labled
                                                       bags & organize
                                                       in freezer basket

            puree
            & pour

            puree
            & pour

                                        store in an
                                        airtight container
                                        & freeze

COOKING SESSION 3 •• AMAZING MISE EN PLACE PLAN

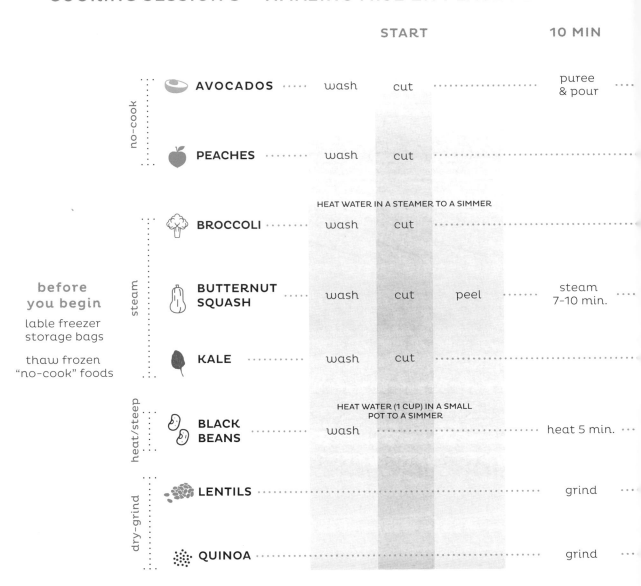

			START			10 MIN
no-cook	AVOCADOS	wash	cut			puree & pour
	PEACHES	wash	cut			
steam	HEAT WATER IN A STEAMER TO A SIMMER					
	BROCCOLI	wash	cut			
	BUTTERNUT SQUASH	wash	cut	peel		steam 7-10 min.
	KALE	wash	cut			
heat/steep	HEAT WATER (1 CUP) IN A SMALL POT TO A SIMMER					
	BLACK BEANS	wash				heat 5 min.
dry-grind	LENTILS					grind
	QUINOA					grind

before you begin

lable freezer storage bags

thaw frozen "no-cook" foods

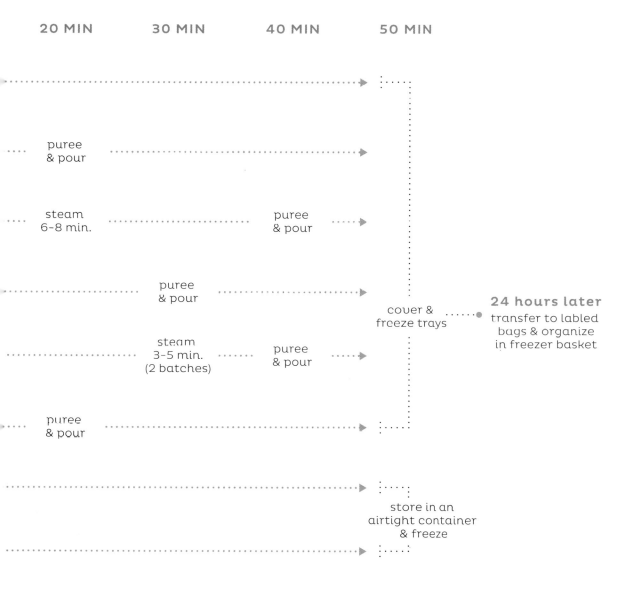

20 MIN **30 MIN** **40 MIN** **50 MIN**

puree
& pour

steam
6-8 min.   puree
                  & pour

puree
& pour

steam   cover &
3-5 min.   puree freeze trays   **24 hours later**
(2 batches) & pour   transfer to labled
                                   bags & organize
                                   in freezer basket

puree
& pour

store in an
airtight container
& freeze

Building Amazing Meals

Once you have prepared the purees and ground whole grain cereals, you are ready to build meals. To effectively use your supply, I recommend meal planning both daily and weekly.

Daily Meal Planning and Thawing Frozen Purees

The best way to prepare for meals is to select meals for baby the night before, according to your weekly menu (described on the following pages). Place frozen puree cubes for each meal in a separate container with a lid and store in the refrigerator overnight to thaw. Meals will be thawed and ready to eat the next day. Purees prepared from recipes in chapter 3 do not require heating and can be consumed cool or at room temperature. If taking meals on-the-go, just grab your prepacked containers right out of the refrigerator. If you do not take the time to thaw frozen puree cubes the night before, you can still thaw cubes on the stove top in a small pot over low heat. Frozen puree cubes may also be microwaved, though I do not personally recommend this approach, as unnecessary nutrient loss may result. Refer to chapter 2 (page 50) for additional thawing information.

Weekly Meal Planning

Meal planning on a weekly basis makes it easier for you to ensure that a well-balanced, diverse assortment of foods is offered. Weekly menu plans should vary each week and become progressively more complex as baby grows and his palate develops. In the early stages of introducing solid food purees, baby will eat just one food per day, one time per day. Eventually, baby will eat three meals per day, with multiple foods at each meal. Every baby is different, so there is no one correct amount or strict advice to give regarding quantity of solid foods. Most babies start off eating one cube at a time, but some may start off eating three cubes at a time! Follow baby's cues. You choose what to feed baby, but let baby decide how much to eat. A sample three-month menu of meals is provided on pages 20–22. When creating weekly menu plans, there are several things to remember.

ONE AT A TIME, THEN COMBINE

Introduce new foods one at a time to screen for allergies. Offer new foods for three to five days before introducing another new food. Once the new food is known to be tolerated, it can be combined with other foods. See chapter 2, page 40, for more details.

FLAVOR AND TEXTURE, COLOR AND NUTRIENTS (FaT CaN)

Baby's meals should be *flavorful*, with the appropriate *texture*, made of whole foods from every *color* of the rainbow, while keeping *nutrients* in mind. Refer to page 41 for more details.

Amazing Three-Month Menu of Meals

Your supply of whole food purees offers the freedom to build your own weekly menus. The following three pages feature a sample three-month menu of 175 increasingly complex meals. This menu uses the 270 fruit, vegetable, and legume puree cubes and cereals created using the Amazing Whole Foods Menu (plus two mix-ins, see page 24), as well as feeding guidelines, including *FaT CaN* and the principle of *one at a time, then combine*.

AMAZING THREE-MONTH MENU OF MEALS

MONTH 1

	Sunday	Monday	Tuesday	Wednesday	Thursday	Friday	Saturday
WEEK 1	sweet potatoes	sweet potatoes	sweet potatoes	sweet potatoes	sweet peas	sweet peas	sweet peas
WEEK 2	bananas	bananas	bananas	butternut squash	butternut squash	butternut squash	butternut squash
WEEK 3	apples	apples	apples	rice cereal + bananas	rice cereal + sweet peas	rice cereal + butternut squash	rice cereal + apples
WEEK 4 ¹	avocados	avocados	avocados	parsnips	parsnips	parsnips	parsnips + rice cereal
²	sweet potatoes + apples	sweet peas + rice cereal	butternut squash + rice cereal	bananas + rice cereal	avocados	sweet peas + rice cereal	butternut squash + apples

Italicized foods indicate foods being introduced as a new food, following the principle of *one at a time, then combine*. Each instance of a whole food appearing on the menu indicates one frozen puree cube of that individual whole food. The numbers at the top left-hand corners indicate which meal is to be eaten: 1 = breakfast, 2 = lunch, 3 = dinner.

MONTH 2

		Sunday	Monday	Tuesday	Wednesday	Thursday	Friday	Saturday
WEEK 5	1	pears	pears	pears	mangoes	mangoes	mangoes	mangoes
	2	avocados	butternut squash + bananas	parsnips + apples	avocados	sweet peas + rice cereal	sweet potatoes + pears	parsnips + rice cereal
WEEK 6	1	broccoli	broccoli + rice cereal	broccoli + rice cereal	broccoli + rice cereal	cherries	cherries	cherries + rice cereal
	2	butternut squash + rice cereal	parsnips + bananas	mangoes + avocados	sweet potatoes + bananas	sweet peas + rice cereal	broccoli + apples	parsnips + pears
WEEK 7	1	oat cereal + bananas	oat cereal + pears	oat cereal + cherries	kale + bananas	kale + apples	kale + sweet potatoes	kale + pears
	2	sweet potatoes + pears	mangoes + cherries	parsnips + apples	broccoli + pears	avocados + mangoes	butternut squash + cherries	mangoes + oat cereal
WEEK 8	1	black beans + rice cereal	black beans + rice cereal	black beans + rice cereal	prunes + oat cereal	prunes + oat cereal	prunes + rice cereal	prunes + rice cereal
	2	avocados + mangoes	sweet peas + sweet potatoes	broccoli + pears	butternut squash + cherries	kale + bananas	sweet potatoes + black beans	parsnips + bananas

MONTH 3

		Sunday	Monday	Tuesday	Wednesday	Thursday	Friday	Saturday
WEEK 9	1	yogurt + bananas	yogurt + mangoes	yogurt + pears	yogurt + prunes	carrots + rice cereal	carrots + kale	carrots + black beans
	2	broccoli + pears	sweet peas + parsnips	kale + prunes	bananas + cherries	broccoli + prunes	cherries + yogurt	prunes + yogurt
	3	butternut squash + kale	avocados + black beans	sweet peas + butternut squash	parsnips + pears	kale + sweet potatoes	broccoli + parsnips	sweet potatoes + sweet peas
WEEK 10	1	peaches + oat cereal	peaches + oat cereal	peaches + oat cereal	haricots verts + rice cereal	haricots verts + rice cereal	haricots verts + rice cereal	haricots verts + carrots
	2	cherries + yogurt	prunes + yogurt	carrots + black beans + apples	cherries + oat cereal + yogurt	carrots + sweet peas	prunes + oat cereal + yogurt	black beans + rice cereal + apples
	3	sweet peas + carrots + rice cereal	kale + carrots + black beans	broccoli + prunes + rice cereal	carrots + broccoli + rice cereal	avocados + mangoes + black beans	kale + butternut squash + rice cereal	peaches + cherries + oat cereal
WEEK 11	1	blueberries + oat cereal	blueberries + oat cereal	blueberries + peaches	red lentils + rice cereal	red lentils + broccoli	red lentils + butternut squash	red lentils + sweet potatoes
	2	haricots verts + peaches + rice cereal	parsnips + prunes + rice cereal	haricots verts + carrots + bananas	peaches + blueberries + yogurt	blueberries + peaches + yogurt	sweet peas + carrots + rice cereal	parsnips + haricots verts + rice cereal
	3	kale + sweet potatoes + black beans	haricots verts + peaches + rice cereal	avocados + mangoes + black beans	broccoli + haricots verts + pears	haricots verts + apples + rice cereal	kale + apples + haricots verts	avocados + mangoes + black beans
WEEK 12	1	quinoa cereal + cherries + blueberries	quinoa cereal + peaches + cherries	quinoa cereal + prunes	flaxseed + blueberries + oat cereal	flaxseed + blueberries + yogurt	flaxseed + blueberries + oat cereal	flaxseed + prunes + oat cereal
	2	blueberries + peaches + yogurt	pears + blueberries + yogurt	blueberries + yogurt + oat cereal	cherries + peaches + oat cereal	peaches + blueberries + oat cereal	peaches + blueberries + oat cereal	peaches + blueberries + yogurt
	3	avocados + mangoes + black beans	kale + carrots + apples + haricots verts	broccoli + prunes + rice cereal	haricots verts + carrots + quinoa cereal	kale + carrots + red lentils + haricots verts	haricots verts + carrots + quinoa cereal	avocados + mangoes + black beans

Mix-Ins

In addition to purees and whole grain cereals, baby's meals can be complemented with a variety of mix-ins. Mix these complementary foods into purees to increase nutrient density, boost flavor, and add texture.

YOGURT

Use full-fat plain yogurt for baby, as prepackaged flavored yogurts are filled with unnecessary added sugars. Mixing plain yogurt with fruit purees (as well as other mix-ins) can easily create sweetened, fully flavored yogurts. Several yogurt styles are available, including regular, Greek, and Skyr (Icelandic), and all are suitable for baby.

METHOD: Combine 1 tablespoon of plain yogurt with any thawed fruit puree cube, and gently mix to combine. You can also add up to 1 tablespoon of cereal and a sprinkle of additional mix-ins (such as flaxseed, wheat germ, or coconut), if desired. When baby is at least twelve months old, try adding a dash of maple syrup for a special treat. Increase quantities of ingredients proportionally as baby's appetite increases.

EGGS

Eggs are one of the most nutritionally dense whole foods available. If you are concerned with egg allergies, offer baby only cooked egg yolks, as the common allergy concern is limited to the protein in egg whites.

METHOD: Starting with one hard-boiled egg (see page 153), carefully separate the cooked egg yolk from the egg white. Smash the cooked egg yolk in a small bowl with the back of a fork until slightly creamy and crumbly. Add the smashed egg yolk to any thawed vegetable or legume puree, and gently mix, combining additional mix-ins (such as herbs, spices, seaweed, and so on), and up to 1 tablespoon of cereal as desired. Rather than discarding the cooked egg whites, incorporate them into an adult meal.

GROUND NUTS AND SEEDS

Nuts and seeds provide a wide assortment of nutrients. Nuts and seeds to choose from include almonds, Brazil nuts, cashew nuts, macadamia nuts, peanuts (technically legumes), pecans, pistachios, walnuts, chia seeds, flaxseeds, hemp seeds, pumpkin seeds (pepitas), sesame seeds, and sunflower seeds. If you are not concerned with allergies (see page 47), then nuts and seeds can safely be given to baby if they are finely ground. A clean coffee grinder works well to pulse small quantities (¼ to ½ cup) of nuts and seeds into a fine powder. A blender or food processor can be used for larger batches. Carefully pulse your processor rather than blend at high speeds, or you may overprocess the nuts or seeds and create a butter. Some nuts and seeds can be purchased preground, and will often be labeled as a "meal" or "flour" (for example, ground flaxseed is commonly labeled as "flax meal," while ground almonds may be labeled as "almond flour"). Always choose nuts and seeds without any added salt or sugar. Due to their highly nutritious oil content, nuts and seeds should be stored in the freezer or refrigerator to prevent rancidity, especially after grinding.

METHOD: Start with ¼ teaspoon of ground nuts or seeds mixed with any thawed puree cube, yogurt, or cereal. Progressively increase the amount as desired.

NUT AND SEED BUTTERS

Nut and seed butters can be safely given to baby when mixed well and thinned out into a puree. (Nut and seed butters can be a choking hazard for baby if they are too thick and sticky.) Use additional water, breast milk, or formula, if necessary. Nut and seed butters can be made out of any nut or seed by sufficiently grinding and pureeing them. Many butters can be purchased, including peanut butter, almond butter, cashew nut butter, sunflower butter, and sesame seed butter (tahini). Bulk sections of some grocery stores also have a "grind your own" butter station. If purchasing premade butters, choose those that are made from only one ingredient: the nut or seed. Premade butters often contain salt, other vegetable oils, and thickeners, which produce excessively thick butters that are more difficult to adequately thin out for baby. Nut and seed butters can be created with a blender at home, but be sure to check the owner's manual before attempting to do so to avoid damaging your machine. (A high-speed blender, such as the Vitamix, can easily and safely create nut and seed butters.)

METHOD: Mix up to 1 tablespoon of any nut or seed butter with any 2 cubes of thawed puree. Mix well with a fork to ensure the butter is adequately thinned out into the puree, adding additional water, breast milk, or formula if necessary.

CHEESES

Cheeses offer a good source of calcium, fat, and protein to complement baby's meals, as well as offering an addition of flavor and texture. Shredded cheeses can easily be mixed and melted into any warmed puree. Take care not to make the puree too thick with melted cheese, to prevent a choking hazard. Wet cheeses, such as cottage cheese and ricotta cheese, are also a convenient mix-in. Avoid raw-milk cheeses, which are made from unpasteurized milk and may contain harmful pathogens.

METHOD: Add up to 1 tablespoon of shredded cheese to 1 thawed and warmed vegetable or legume puree cube, and gently mix to melt the cheese. Add 1 tablespoon of cottage cheese or ricotta cheese to 1 thawed fruit, vegetable, or legume puree cube, and gently mix until combined.

MEAT AND FISH

While it is possible to puree meats and fish for baby, I prefer not to, as pureeing cooked meat results in a sticky paste that is rather unappetizing to the senses. I prefer to save the introduction of meat and fish for when baby is ready to accept its texture in small pieces. Meat or fish should always be thoroughly cooked (see page 50). All cooked meat should be cut across the grain and served in pieces no larger than ¼ inch in any direction. To be efficient, offer baby meat that has already been cooked from the family meal. Ground, shredded, or finely diced meats (beef, turkey, chicken, lamb, pork, fish) are the most appropriate textures. Always remove all bones and skin. Do not offer processed deli meats, which are typically high in salt, nitrates, and other preservatives.

METHOD: Mix up to 1 tablespoon of cooked meat with any thawed vegetable, legume, or fruit puree cube. Include up to 1 tablespoon of cereal, as well as any other mix-ins, such as herbs, spices, or cheese, if desired.

WHEAT GERM

Wheat germ is the most nutrient-dense part of the wheat kernel. When wheat is milled to create white flour, the germ is removed from the wheat kernel (along with the bran), which is why white flours are considered less nutritious than whole wheat. Wheat germ is a particularly excellent source of vitamin E. Sprinkle it on any baby food puree. Find wheat germ in the baking or bulk section of most supermarkets. Due to its highly nutritious oil content, wheat germ will readily go rancid, so check the use-by date before purchasing, and store in the refrigerator to extend shelf life.

METHOD: Start with ¼ teaspoon of wheat germ and mix with any puree, yogurt, or cereal. Progressively increase the amount as desired.

NUTRITIONAL YEAST

Nutritional yeast is an inactive yeast full of B vitamins and minerals. It is made from the yeast *Saccharomyces cerevisiae*, which is grown on molasses, then harvested, washed, and dried with heat to "inactivate" it. Nutritional yeast is not the same as brewer's, baker's, or Torula yeast (none of which should be substituted for each other). Some nutritional yeast is fortified with vitamin B12 (check the label to confirm), making this a staple in the diet of many vegans. The flavor of nutritional yeast can be described as nutty, cheesy, savory, and umami. Nutritional yeast can be found in a flake or powder form in the bulk or dried goods section of any health food store and some supermarkets.

METHOD: Start with ¼ teaspoon of nutritional yeast mixed with any puree, yogurt, or cereal. Progressively increase the amount as desired.

DRIED SEAWEED

Dried seaweed contains many minerals. There are several different types of seaweed (sea vegetables), but the easiest to incorporate into baby's food is nori, a common seaweed used to roll sushi. To prepare ground seaweed, tear 1 to 2 sheets of nori into pieces and grind in a coffee grinder or small bowl of a food processor. Alternatively, chop nori sheets with a knife until finely crumbled. Nori has a naturally salty and umami flavor profile. It can be found in the Asian section of most supermarkets.

METHOD: Start with ¼ teaspoon of ground dried seaweed mixed with any puree or cereal. Progressively increase amount as desired.

COCONUT

Coconuts offer a wonderful natural source of fat, fiber, and minerals. Fresh, whole coconuts are particularly flavorful, but they can be extremely difficult to handle, so I recommend dried, unsweetened, finely shredded coconut, with no additional ingredients (such as sulfites or sugar). If you cannot find finely shredded coconut, you can use your blender or food processor to create finer shreds from regularly shredded coconut or coconut flakes. Dried coconut can be found in the bulk or baking section of most supermarkets.

METHOD: Start with ¼ teaspoon of finely shredded coconut mixed with any puree, yogurt, or cereal. Progressively increase the amount as desired.

HERBS AND SPICES

Baby's meals can be mildly seasoned with dried herbs and spices (excluding salt; see page 42).

Cinnamon, nutmeg, mint, oregano, ginger, cumin, and curry powder are all tasty examples to try. Finely chopped fresh herbs can also be used. Incorporate the flavors you typically cook with in your kitchen.

METHOD: Start with just a pinch (⅛ teaspoon) of herbs or spices (dried or fresh), mixed into any puree, yogurt, or cereal. Progressively increase the amount as desired.

Traveling and On-the-Go

Baby food options become a bit more limited when traveling or on-the-go. Although you are not likely to have the same variety of foods and tools available to you when you travel, there are some strategies you can use to feed baby fresh whole foods without resorting to processed jarred or pouched food.

If you are just going to be out for the day or taking a short road trip, you can easily pack baby's food and take it with you. Frozen or thawed purees (which do not contain meat, fish, dairy, or eggs) can be stored in a cooler and fed to baby at a cool or room temperature. Another tip is to bring an avocado or banana with you (or pick one up at a local store while on the road), which you can easily smash into a puree with the back of a fork. My babies ate a lot of bananas and avocados when we were on-the-go, due to their convenience!

If you will be traveling for more than one day, you will need to have a plan for preparing baby food while away from home. A great tool is an immersion blender. Immersion blenders are compact, so they can easily be packed in your luggage bag. If you have access to fresh whole foods (and an electrical outlet), you can purchase local produce and prepare baby food as you need it. You may not have your freezer basket full of foods to mix and match, but you can very quickly whip up breakfast by blending a banana and a handful of blueberries, or a nectarine with raspberries. Remember that the easiest, fastest purees to make are the "no-cook" recipes in this book. An immersion blender, however, will not likely be able to make a smooth puree out of leafy greens. For more variety in baby's travel menu, pack canned beans or whole grain flours from which you can prepare cereals if you have access to a stove. Plain yogurt is another food to purchase when you arrive at your location. Add yogurt to any fruit puree to create a more filling meal.

If you feel overwhelmed, or unable to make baby food while traveling, do not despair, and do not feel guilty. Traveling is energy intensive, and traveling with a baby can be nothing short of exhausting. A few days' worth of processed baby food will do no harm if you feel the need to resort to it. You will be home before you know it, and baby will gladly be back to the healthy routine of consuming homemade whole foods.

Flavor Compatibility Guide

Use the following Flavor Compatibility Guide as a reference for combining whole foods for optimal flavor when building meals. It was designed for each whole food featured in the Simple Puree Recipes (chapter 3). These lists are a general guide and by no means comprehensive, so feel free to be adventurous and create your own combinations.

Multiple whole foods within any given category can be combined. Start by combining frozen puree cubes within any category in a 1:1 ratio. For example, by looking at the Apples category, you will see that 1 puree cube of apples can be combined with 1 puree cube of carrots. For a more complex meal, 1 puree cube of kale can also be added.

If you find that baby does not like a given meal combination due to particularly strong flavors, adding a cube of fruit for enhanced sweetness often does the trick. Include any of the mix-ins discussed earlier for additional flavor.

APPLES

Apricots • Avocados • Bananas • Beets • Black beans
Blackberries • Blueberries • Broccoli • Cannellini beans
Cantaloupe • Carrots • Cauliflower • Chard • Cherries
Figs • Garbanzo beans • Green beans/Haricots verts
Honeydew melon • Kale • Kidney beans • Kiwifruit
Lentils • Mangoes • Navy beans • Nectarines
Northern beans • Papaya • Parsnips • Peaches • Pears
Pinto beans • Plums/Prunes • Raspberries • Spinach
Split peas • Strawberries • Summer squash
Sweet peas • Sweet potatoes • Turnips
Whole grains • Winter squash

APRICOTS

Apples • Bananas • Blackberries • Blueberries • Carrots
Cherries • Mangoes • Nectarines • Papaya • Peaches
Pears • Plums/Prunes • Raspberries • Strawberries
Whole grains

ASPARAGUS

Bananas • Carrots • Cauliflower • Parsnips • Spinach
Summer squash • Sweet peas • Whole grains

AVOCADOS

Apples • Bananas • Beets • Black beans • Blackberries
Blueberries • Cantaloupe • Honeydew melon
Mangoes • Nectarines • Papaya • Peaches • Pears
Pinto beans • Raspberries • Strawberries • Whole grains

BANANAS

Apples • Apricots • Asparagus • Avocados • Blackberries
Blueberries • Broccoli • Cantaloupe • Carrots
Cauliflower • Chard • Cherries • Figs
Green beans/Haricots verts • Honeydew melon • Kale
Kiwifruit • Mangoes • Nectarines • Papaya • Parsnips
Peaches • Pears • Plums/Prunes • Raspberries
Spinach • Split peas • Strawberries • Summer squash
Sweet peas • Sweet potatoes • Watermelon
Whole grains • Winter squash

BEETS

Apples • Avocados • Carrots • Edamame
Garbanzo beans • Parsnips • Pears • Sweet potatoes
Whole grains • Winter squash

BLACK BEANS

Apples • Avocado • Carrots • Mangoes • Papaya
Parsnips • Pears • Summer squash • Sweet potatoes
Whole grains • Winter squash

BLACKBERRIES

Apples • Apricots • Avocados • Bananas • Blueberries
Cantaloupe • Carrots • Figs • Honeydew melon
Kiwifruit • Mangoes • Nectarines • Papaya • Peaches
Pears • Plums/Prunes • Raspberries • Strawberries
Watermelon • Whole grains

BLUEBERRIES

Apples • Apricots • Avocados • Bananas
Blackberries • Cantaloupe • Carrots • Cherries • Figs
Honeydew melon • Kiwifruit • Mangoes • Nectarines
Papaya • Peaches • Pears • Plums/Prunes • Raspberries
Spinach • Strawberries • Watermelon • Whole grains

BROCCOLI

Apples • Bananas • Cannellini beans • Carrots
Cauliflower • Garbanzo beans • Lentils • Navy beans
Northern beans • Parsnips • Pears • Plums/Prunes
Sweet potatoes • Whole grains • Winter squash

CANNELLINI BEANS

Apples • Broccoli • Carrots • Cauliflower • Chard
Kale • Parsnips • Pears • Spinach • Summer squash
Sweet potatoes • Whole grains • Winter squash

CANTALOUPE

Apples • Avocados • Bananas • Blackberries
Blueberries • Honeydew melon • Kiwifruit • Mangoes
Papaya • Pears • Raspberries • Strawberries
Watermelon • Whole grains

CARROTS

Apples • Apricots • Asparagus • Bananas • Beets
Black beans • Blackberries • Blueberries • Broccoli
Cannellini beans • Cauliflower • Chard • Edamame
Garbanzo beans • Green beans/Haricots verts
Kale • Kidney beans • Lentils • Navy beans
Northern beans • Parsnips • Pears • Pinto beans
Plums/Prunes • Raspberries • Spinach • Split peas
Summer squash • Sweet peas • Sweet potatoes
Turnips • Whole grains • Winter squash

CAULIFLOWER

Apples • Asparagus • Bananas • Broccoli
Cannellini beans • Carrots • Chard • Edamame
Garbanzo beans • Kale • Kidney beans • Lentils
Navy beans • Northern beans • Parsnips • Pears
Plums/Prunes • Spinach • Split peas • Sweet peas
Sweet potatoes • Whole grains • Winter squash

CHARD

Apples • Bananas • Cannellini beans • Carrots
Cauliflower • Garbanzo beans • Lentils • Navy beans
Northern beans • Parsnips • Peaches • Pears
Plums/Prunes • Strawberries • Sweet potatoes
Whole grains • Winter squash

CHERRIES

Apples • Apricots • Bananas • Blueberries
Kiwifruit • Mangoes • Nectarines • Papaya • Peaches
Pears • Plums/Prunes • Summer squash
Whole grains • Winter squash

EDAMAME

Beets • Carrots • Cauliflower • Parsnips
Summer squash • Sweet potatoes
Whole grains • Winter squash

FIGS

Apples • Bananas • Blackberries • Blueberries
Pears • Raspberries • Strawberries • Whole grains

GARBANZO BEANS

Apples • Beets • Broccoli • Carrots
Cauliflower • Chard • Kale • Parsnips • Pears
Spinach • Summer squash • Sweet potatoes
Whole grains • Winter squash

GREEN BEANS/HARICOTS VERTS

Apples • Bananas • Carrots • Nectarines • Parsnips
Peaches • Pears • Summer squash • Sweet potatoes
Whole grains • Winter squash

HONEYDEW MELON

Apples • Avocados • Bananas • Blackberries
Blueberries • Cantaloupe • Kiwifruit • Mangoes
Papaya • Pears • Raspberries • Strawberries
Watermelon • Whole grains

KALE

Apples • Bananas • Cannellini beans • Carrots
Cauliflower • Garbanzo beans • Lentils
Navy beans • Northern beans • Parsnips
Peaches • Pears • Plums/Prunes • Strawberries
Sweet potatoes • Whole grains • Winter squash

KIDNEY BEANS

Apples • Carrots • Cauliflower • Parsnips
Pears • Summer squash • Sweet potatoes
Whole grains • Winter squash

KIWIFRUIT

Apples • Bananas • Blackberries
Blueberries • Cantaloupe • Cherries • Honeydew melon
Mangoes • Papaya • Pears • Plums/Prunes • Raspberries
Strawberries • Watermelon • Whole grains

LENTILS

Apples • Broccoli • Carrots • Cauliflower • Chard
Kale • Parsnips • Pears • Spinach • Summer squash
Sweet potatoes • Whole grains • Winter squash

MANGOES

Apples • Apricots • Avocados • Bananas
Black beans • Blackberries • Blueberries • Cantaloupe
Cherries • Honeydew melon • Kiwifruit • Nectarines
Papaya • Peaches • Pears • Pinto beans
Plums/Prunes • Raspberries • Strawberries
Watermelon • Whole grains

NAVY BEANS

Apples • Broccoli • Carrots • Cauliflower • Chard
Kale • Parsnips • Pears • Spinach • Summer squash
Sweet potatoes • Whole grains • Winter squash

NECTARINES

Apples • Apricots • Avocados • Bananas • Blackberries
Blueberries • Cherries • Green beans/Haricots verts
Mangoes • Papaya • Peaches • Pears • Plums/Prunes
Raspberries • Strawberries • Summer squash
Watermelon • Whole grains

NORTHERN BEANS

Apples • Broccoli • Carrots • Cauliflower • Chard
Kale • Parsnips • Pears • Spinach • Summer squash
Sweet potatoes • Whole grains • Winter squash

PAPAYA

Apples • Apricots • Avocados • Bananas • Black beans
Blackberries • Blueberries • Cantaloupe • Cherries
Honeydew melon • Kiwifruit • Mangoes • Nectarines
Peaches • Pears • Pinto beans • Plums/Prunes
Raspberries • Strawberries • Watermelon • Whole grains

PARSNIPS

Apples • Asparagus • Bananas • Beets • Black beans
Broccoli • Cannellini beans • Carrots • Cauliflower
Chard • Edamame • Garbanzo beans
Green beans/Haricots verts • Kale • Kidney beans
Lentils • Navy beans • Northern beans • Pears
Pinto beans • Plums/Prunes • Spinach • Split peas
Summer squash • Sweet peas • Sweet potatoes
Turnips • Whole grains • Winter squash

PEACHES

Apples • Apricots • Avocados • Bananas
Blackberries • Blueberries • Chard • Cherries
Green beans/Haricots verts • Kale • Mangoes
Nectarines • Papaya • Pears • Plums/Prunes
Raspberries • Spinach • Strawberries
Summer squash • Watermelon • Whole grains

PEARS

Apples • Apricots • Avocados • Bananas • Beets
Black beans • Blackberries • Blueberries • Broccoli
Cannellini beans • Cantaloupe • Carrots • Cauliflower
Chard • Cherries • Figs • Garbanzo beans
Green beans/Haricots verts • Honeydew melon
Kale • Kidney beans • Kiwifruit • Lentils • Mangoes
Navy beans • Nectarines • Northern beans • Papaya
Parsnips • Peaches • Pinto beans • Plums/Prunes
Raspberries • Spinach • Split peas • Strawberries
Summer squash • Sweet peas • Sweet potatoes
Turnips • Whole grains • Winter squash

PINTO BEANS

Apples • Avocados • Carrots • Mangoes • Papaya
Parsnips • Pears • Summer squash • Sweet potatoes
Whole grains • Winter squash

PLUMS/PRUNES

Apples • Apricots • Bananas • Blackberries
Blueberries • Broccoli • Carrots • Cauliflower
Chard • Cherries • Kale • Kiwifruit • Mangoes
Nectarines • Papaya • Parsnips • Peaches • Pears
Raspberries • Spinach • Strawberries • Whole grains

RASPBERRIES

Apples • Apricots • Avocados • Bananas • Blackberries
Blueberries • Cantaloupe • Carrots • Figs
Honeydew melon • Kiwifruit • Mangoes • Nectarines
Papaya • Peaches • Pears • Plums/Prunes • Spinach
Strawberries • Watermelon • Whole grains

SPINACH

Apples • Asparagus • Bananas • Blueberries
Cannellini beans • Carrots • Cauliflower
Garbanzo beans • Lentils • Navy beans
Northern beans • Parsnips • Peaches • Pears
Plums/Prunes • Raspberries • Strawberries
Sweet potatoes • Whole grains • Winter squash

SPLIT PEAS

Apples • Bananas • Carrots • Cauliflower • Parsnips
Pears • Summer squash • Sweet potatoes • Turnips
Whole grains • Winter squash

STRAWBERRIES

Apples • Apricots • Avocados • Bananas
Blackberries • Blueberries • Cantaloupe • Chard
Figs • Honeydew melon • Kale • Kiwifruit
Mangoes • Nectarines • Papaya • Peaches • Pears
Plums/Prunes • Raspberries • Spinach
Watermelon • Whole grains

SUMMER SQUASH

Apples • Asparagus • Bananas • Black beans
Cannellini beans • Carrots • Cherries • Edamame
Garbanzo beans • Green beans/Haricots verts
Kidney beans • Lentils • Navy beans • Nectarines
Northern beans • Parsnips • Peaches • Pears
Pinto beans • Split peas • Sweet peas
Sweet potatoes • Whole grains • Winter squash

SWEET PEAS

Apples • Asparagus • Bananas • Carrots • Cauliflower
Parsnips • Pears • Summer squash • Sweet potatoes
Turnips • Whole grains • Winter squash

SWEET POTATOES

Apples • Bananas • Beets • Black beans
Broccoli • Cannellini beans • Carrots • Cauliflower
Chard • Edamame • Garbanzo beans
Green beans/Haricots verts • Kale
Kidney beans • Lentils • Navy beans
Northern beans • Parsnips • Pears
Pinto beans • Spinach • Split peas
Summer squash • Sweet peas
Turnips • Whole grains

TURNIPS

Apples • Carrots • Parsnips • Pears
Split peas • Sweet peas • Sweet potatoes
Whole grains • Winter squash

WATERMELON

Bananas • Blackberries • Blueberries • Cantaloupe
Honeydew melon • Mangoes • Nectarines • Papaya
Peaches • Raspberries • Strawberries • Whole grains

WINTER SQUASH

Apples • Bananas • Beets • Black beans • Broccoli
Cannellini beans • Carrots • Cauliflower • Chard
Cherries • Edamame • Garbanzo beans
Green beans/Haricots verts • Kale • Kidney beans
Lentils • Navy beans • Northern beans • Parsnips
Pears • Pinto beans • Spinach • Split peas
Summer squash • Sweet peas • Turnips • Whole grains

CHAPTER 2

before you begin

••

The general information and specific guidelines provided in this chapter will give you a solid background before beginning your first cooking session or feeding baby. You will find tips on when— and how—to introduce solid foods safely, along with a handy timeline with all the milestones to keep in mind. Information on screening for allergies and keeping things clean in the kitchen will help you keep baby safe and sound during the feeding process. Finally, tips on selecting and preparing whole foods will inspire you to use your senses and choose the best ingredients throughout the year.

Feeding Timeline and Guidelines

These simple feeding guidelines and timeline will give you a well-rounded vision of how to responsibly feed your baby.

Introducing Solid Foods

When babies should start eating solid food as well as what and how much they should eat are among the first things to know.

WHEN TO START

The American Academy of Pediatrics (AAP) and World Health Organization (WHO) currently recommend that solid food be introduced at around six months of age. Some pediatricians recommend starting solid foods at four to six months, while others recommend waiting the full six months. Introducing solid foods earlier than four months of age may interfere with baby's ability to consume adequate nutrients and calories due to prematurely displacing breast milk or formula, and may increase the risk of developing food allergies. On the other hand, delaying introduction of solid foods beyond the age of six months may lead to adverse consequences, including decreased growth, because baby may no longer obtain adequate calories from breast milk or formula alone; iron deficiency anemia, due to depletion of natural iron stores; and a resistance from baby to trying solid foods, which often comes with an aversion to texture.

Around six months, infants should also be able to

- Sit upright with support and have good head and neck control.

- Display readiness for varied textures by placing hands and/or toys in their mouth.

- Open their mouth and lean forward when offered food.

- Lean back and turn away when uninterested in food.

- Have the ability to swallow food that is placed in their mouth instead of pushing it out. (Infants have an extrusion reflex that usually disappears at four to five months of age.)

ORDER OF INTRODUCTION

The introduction of solid foods during the first year of life has varied over time and across cultures. Recommendations still vary today because many are based more on tradition than on scientific evidence. In the United States, cereals, fruits, and vegetables are generally introduced first, followed by legumes, then dairy (yogurt, cheeses) and meats. Other cultures introduce dairy or meat first. The order of introduction does not necessarily matter; the goal should be to gradually get baby to consume a diet filled with a wide variety of healthy whole foods. Specialty diets that eliminate specific food categories, including vegetarian, vegan, or gluten-free diets, can safely be designed for baby with proper planning (see Appendix A on page 171).

ONE AT A TIME, THEN COMBINE

Introduce only one new food at a time to screen for allergies (see "Allergies and Food Intolerances," page 47). Offer an individual food for three to five days before introducing a new food. An initial allergic reaction—symptoms range from a mild rash to difficulty breathing—may take three to five days to appear. Once it has been determined that a food is well tolerated, feel free to combine it with other foods, including new foods. See the sample three-month menu of meals utilizing this approach provided on pages 20–22.

WATER

Once baby starts eating solid foods, offer water as well. Give baby her own sippy cup filled with water and make it available during solid food feedings. Breast milk or formula will keep baby sufficiently hydrated, but baby should start learning the skill of self-quenching thirst around the age of six months.

FOODS TO LIMIT OR AVOID

Some foods are not appropriate for baby to consume during the initial phases of eating solids. Carefully monitor intake of the following foods.

HONEY AND CORN SYRUP: Honey and corn syrup may contain spores of *Clostridium botulinum*, which can cause botulism in infants because their digestive systems are not mature enough to prevent the growth of these spores.

Completely avoid honey and corn syrup prior to twelve months of age.

COW'S MILK: Cow's milk, which contains specific proteins and fats that are difficult for infants to digest and absorb, should not be introduced before twelve months of age. Breast milk or formula should be the exclusive source of milk until this time. Other dairy products containing cow's milk (yogurt, cheeses) are fine in moderate quantities because these hard-to-digest components are significantly decreased during the process of culturing.

RAW-MILK CHEESES: Raw-milk cheeses are made from unpasteurized milk, which may contain very harmful pathogens (*E. coli* O157:H7, *Listeria*, *Salmonella*), particularly for infants and children. Completely avoid raw-milk cheeses until at least the age of five years.

HIGH-ACID FRUITS: Citrus fruits, tomatoes, pineapple, and strawberries are highly acidic fruits that can cause food sensitivities, such as severe diaper rash for some infants. Baby is typically better able to digest these after twelve months of age.

HIGH-NITRATE VEGETABLES: Infants younger than six months of age cannot properly digest nitrates due to their immature digestive systems. Natural food sources of nitrates include root vegetables (like beets, carrots, and parsnips), green beans, dark leafy green vegetables (like spinach, kale, and chard), broccoli, and cauliflower. For more information on nitrates, see page 172.

HIGH-MERCURY FISH: Infants and children younger than five years of age are advised to entirely avoid fish containing high levels of mercury, including shark, swordfish, tilefish, king mackerel, ahi and bigeye tuna, orange roughy, and marlin, which can harm their developing nervous systems. Safe to consume are the lowest-mercury-level fish and shellfish—shrimp, salmon, pollock, catfish, tilapia, crab (domestic), butterfish, haddock, perch (ocean), sole, trout, whitefish, whiting, scallops, squid (calamari), crawfish/crayfish, herring, mullet, sardines, anchovies, and wild salmon (farmed salmon may contain PCBs (polychlorinated biphenyls), chemicals with serious long-term health effects). For more information on mercury, see page 173.

JUICE: Juices should play a limited part in baby's diet. Rely on whole fruits for meeting nutrient needs, which contain fiber to help control blood sugar. When given in excess, juices can contribute to significant sugar and calorie consumption, as well as cause diarrhea and tooth decay. Juices should not be given at all prior to six months of age. They should be regarded as a treat and should be labeled as 100 percent juice.

HOW MUCH SOLID FOOD

For the first year of life, breast milk or formula should continue to be baby's primary source of nutrition. Baby will start out eating as little as 1 to 2 tablespoons of solid food at a time. Initially, baby should eat solid food only once per day, as eating is only for practice at this point. Solid food should be given after, not before, breast milk or formula so baby does not lose interest in milk. When baby seems hungrier more often, or is not satisfied after a breast milk or formula feeding, gradually increase the frequency of solid food feedings and the amount offered at each meal. Breast milk or formula feedings will naturally decline as solid foods become increasingly more important. Every baby is different, so there is no single correct amount or timeline. You decide what baby will eat, but let baby decide whether and how much to eat. Follow baby's cues, and never force baby to finish a meal. Infants and young children know how to self-regulate eating much better than most adults do. By the time baby is twelve months old, she should be eating three solid meals per day plus one to two snacks.

Flavor and Texture, Color and Nutrients

Keep in mind four key food attributes as the adventure of feeding baby solid food begins: *Flavor* and *Texture*, *Color* and *Nutrients* (*FaT CaN*). To remember *FaT CaN*, think "*fat can be healthy.*" If baby's meals are *flavorful*, with the appropriate *texture*, and if you offer whole foods from every *color* of the rainbow, while keeping *nutrients* in mind, you will provide consistently well-balanced meals.

FLAVOR

Whole foods burst with their own unique flavors. Baby may not like all flavors when initially introduced to them, but do not let that discourage you. New foods may need to be introduced as many as ten times for acceptability to develop. And remember, if baby is given the full opportunity to develop a taste for fresh fruits and vegetables, these preferences will follow her through life. Studies have shown that lifetime flavor preferences are established by the age of three years. Never assume that baby will only be interested in bland foods. In fact, breast-fed babies have already been exposed to a wide array of flavors through breast milk (an underappreciated benefit of breast-feeding). Garlic and broccoli, both relatively strongly flavored foods, were and still are loved by all three of my children, probably in part because I ate a ton of these foods while breast-feeding.

When the solid food eating experience begins, baby will initially be introduced to single whole foods. As eating progresses, these foods can then be combined to provide more flavor depth and a more nutritionally balanced meal. Whole foods can also be strategically paired to mellow strong flavors that baby does not accept. For example, pairing bananas with broccoli will allow the natural sweetness of bananas to detract from broccoli's strong, sulfurous flavor profile (see the Flavor Compatibility Guide, page 31).

If desired, you can mildly season purees with herbs and spices. Just remember *one at a time, then combine*, in order to screen for potential allergies. When introducing seasonings, start with very small quantities (just a pinch), and always taste food before offering to baby. Cinnamon and nutmeg are usually well received. Also try bolder flavors such as curry spices, oregano, and ginger. Avoid adding sugar or salt. Babies have a natural affinity and preference for sugar and will quickly reject sugar-void foods. Salt causes unnecessary strain on her little developing kidneys and builds her palate's tolerance for it.

TEXTURE

As important as flavor is, controlling texture is even more important during the initial phases of introducing solid foods. If the texture is too thick or lumpy, baby will likely immediately reject the food. Initial solid foods should have a very thin, liquid-like consistency. As baby learns to incorporate a chewing motion, she can progress to thicker, chunkier foods. Babies will vary widely on their readiness for texture changes but are typically ready for some lumpiness or chunkiness by seven to eight months of age.

If a puree is too thick, thin it with water, breast milk, or formula. If it is too chunky, puree it further. Conversely, if a puree is too thin, thicken it with cereals (prepared ground grains) or plain yogurt, or pair it with a thicker food. When baby is ready for thicker, chunkier foods, thin purees can be mixed with whole grains (such as oatmeal, couscous, quinoa, and pasta), lentils, split peas, cottage cheese, plain yogurt, tiny pieces of meat, or many other combinations.

Encourage progressive textures throughout the developing eating experience. If you wait too long to move from ultrasmooth purees to chunky foods, baby may develop a texture aversion, which can be challenging to outgrow.

COLOR

The colors of whole foods typically reflect the different *phytonutrients* they contain, such as carotenoids (orange carrots), anthocyanins (deep blue blueberries), and lycopene (red tomatoes and watermelon). Phytonutrients (also called phytochemicals) are organic components of plants that act as antioxidants, enhance immune response, repair DNA damage, cause cancer cells to die, detoxify carcinogens, and more. They destroy free radicals that are encountered in the environment and during the digestion of some foods. Phytonutrients form part of the immune system of plants and function to protect them from diseases, injuries, insects, pollutants, drought, excessive heat, and ultraviolet rays. Since organic plants have to fight harder than conventional

(nonorganic) plants to protect themselves from these environmental stresses (because they have not been treated with commercial pesticides and other chemicals to "protect" them), organic plants typically have higher concentrations of phytonutrients.

Some of the most common types are carotenoids, phenols, polyphenols, anthocyanins, flavones, isoflavones, terpenes, and phytosterols. Brighter and bolder plant colors generally correspond to more concentrated phytonutrients. Since each phytonutrient provides unique beneficial functions to the human body, offer baby whole foods from every color of the rainbow.

NUTRIENTS

For the first year of life, breast milk or formula should be baby's primary source of nutrition. Solid foods will incrementally take a larger place in baby's diet, and as she approaches her first birthday it becomes very important to understand how to meet her nutritional needs predominantly through solid foods. Meticulously calculating amounts of individual nutrients consumed is not necessary (unless advised by your pediatrician to do so). Follow the simple guidelines below to feed baby a nutrient-rich, balanced diet. Refer to Appendix A (page 164) for additional nutrition information, including a detailed discussion of specific nutrients and their food sources as well as a nutrient chart on page 169.

Offer Whole Foods

Nature provides everything baby needs. Baby's diet should be mainly composed of a wide variety of whole foods, including fruits, vegetables, legumes, nuts, seeds, whole grains, meats, fish, dairy, and eggs. Dietary supplements and fortified products are rarely needed when a diverse selection of whole foods form the foundation of a healthy diet.

Omitting food groups from baby's diet should only be done with careful consideration. Vegetarian, vegan, and gluten-free diets are discussed on pages 171–72.

Limit Processed Foods

Processed foods are basically anything other than whole foods. Processed foods usually come in packages and are made with a long list of chemically deconstructed ingredients, many of which are not appropriate for baby's body to digest. Many processed foods (even organic versions) marketed as "kid" foods and drinks tend to be high in refined sugars and are generally nutrient poor. Processed foods should be limited, particularly because they displace natural whole foods in baby's diet.

Do Not Restrict Dietary Fat and Calories During the First Two Years of Life

Fats are an especially important source of calories and nutrients for infants' and toddlers' rapidly growing bodies and developing brains. Remember: *FaT CaN* be healthy! This is specifically true when fat is obtained from whole foods and consumed as part of a balanced diet.

Pay Attention to Protein

In addition to being an essential macronutrient for many of the body's functions and development, adequate protein will help keep baby's blood sugar levels regulated and result in increased satiety and sustained energy. Incorporate some form of protein at every meal (breast milk or formula should remain baby's main source of protein during the first year). However, not all proteins are created equal. The building blocks of proteins are called amino acids, and protein sources are considered "complete" if they supply all essential amino acids in adequate amounts and "incomplete" if they do not. Complete proteins can be readily found in animal products (meats, dairy, eggs) but in few plant sources (only soybeans and quinoa). Certain plant proteins can be combined, however, to yield a complete supply of amino acids (see Appendix A, page 165).

Pay Attention to Iron

Babies are born with a natural storage supply of iron that is typically depleted by six months of age. Iron must then be adequately consumed from solid foods to avoid iron deficiency anemia, the most common nutritional deficiency among infants. Iron from meat sources is much more readily absorbed than iron from plant sources. When relying on plant sources, pairing the iron source with a vitamin C–rich food will greatly enhance absorption (see Appendix A, page 165).

Pay Attention to Calcium

When breast milk or formula consumption significantly declines, usually by baby's first birthday, food sources of calcium should be included to ensure optimal development of bones and teeth as well as for muscle, heart, and digestive health (see Appendix A, page 165).

Health Concerns When Feeding Baby

When baby begins eating solid foods, there are specific health concerns to consider and be aware of.

Choking

Baby has a very small airway. Choking is a common cause of death in children under age one, and the danger remains significant until the age of five.

- Always supervise eating so you can assist if baby chokes.

- Keep baby seated upright, preferably in a high chair, and do not allow baby to lie down, walk, run, or play while eating.

- Teach baby to take small bites and to chew completely.

- Finger foods should be cut no larger than ¼ inch in any direction. Small, circular foods, such as grapes, should be quartered, blueberries should be halved, and so on. If allergies are not a concern (see "Allergies and Food Intolerances," page 47), then nuts can safely be given to baby if they are finely ground in a food processor, blender, or clean coffee grinder.

- Spread sticky foods, such as peanut butter or nut butters, very thinly on toast, crackers, veggies, or fruit.

Coughing is a natural response for trying to dislodge something stuck in the throat. If baby is coughing, allow and encourage her to do so to dislodge the object. Do not try to remove a foreign object unless you can actually see it—you could push it farther into the airway. If baby makes no sounds and appears not to be breathing, she is truly choking and you will need to assist. Set aside time to take an infant and child CPR course. To find a class in your area, visit the American Red Cross website (www.redcross.org).

TIMELINE AND MILESTONES FOR FEEDING BABY

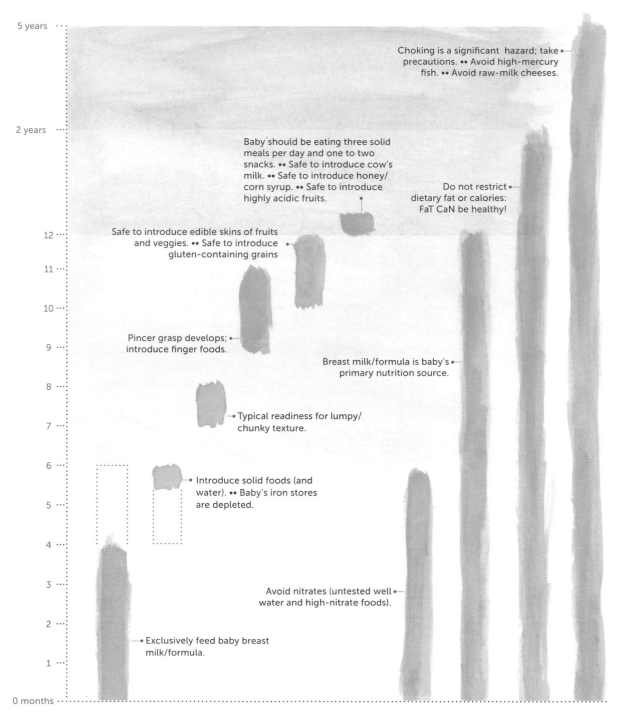

5 years

Choking is a significant hazard; take precautions. •• Avoid high-mercury fish. •• Avoid raw-milk cheeses.

2 years

Baby should be eating three solid meals per day and one to two snacks. •• Safe to introduce cow's milk. •• Safe to introduce honey/corn syrup. •• Safe to introduce highly acidic fruits.

Do not restrict dietary fat or calories: FaT CaN be healthy!

12

Safe to introduce edible skins of fruits and veggies. •• Safe to introduce gluten-containing grains

11

10

9

Pincer grasp develops; introduce finger foods.

Breast milk/formula is baby's primary nutrition source.

8

7

Typical readiness for lumpy/chunky texture.

6

Introduce solid foods (and water). •• Baby's iron stores are depleted.

5

4

3

Avoid nitrates (untested well water and high-nitrate foods).

2

1

Exclusively feed baby breast milk/formula.

0 months

Allergies and Food Intolerances

Food allergies and intolerances can cause not only discomfort but also potentially life-threatening conditions. Care must be taken to monitor and intervene if any such reaction occurs.

ALLERGIES

When baby begins eating solid foods, introduce individual foods one at a time in order to screen for food allergies. New foods should be offered for three to five days (which is how long it could take for an allergic reaction to appear) before introducing another new food. Remember: *one at a time, then combine.*

According to the American Academy of Allergy, Asthma, and Immunology, approximately 8 percent of children will develop a food allergy. Infants are at greatest risk for developing food allergies if they already have an atopic disease (asthma, eczema), or if either parent or a sibling has allergies or other atopic diseases. A food allergy causes an immune system reaction that affects numerous organs in the body. In most cases, food allergies are mild, but in rare cases they can be severe, sometimes triggering life-threatening conditions. If a food allergy is present, even a tiny amount of the offending food can cause an immediate reaction. Many different foods can trigger an allergic reaction, but the following eight foods or groups of foods are responsible 90 percent of the time:

1. Cow's milk
2. Eggs
3. Fish
4. Peanuts
5. Shellfish
6. Soy
7. Tree nuts
8. Wheat

Common signs of an allergic reaction include, but are not limited to:

- Hives
- Rash
- Difficulty breathing
- Face, tongue, or lip swelling
- Wheezing
- Vomiting
- Diarrhea
- Gassiness

The American Academy of Pediatrics (AAP) previously recommended in its 2000 feeding guidelines that parents delay or avoid feeding infants and young children some of these highly allergenic foods to help prevent the possible development of food allergies. The AAP revised its guidelines in 2008, however, after finding that there is no convincing evidence that avoiding these foods during the early months and years will prevent food allergies. The AAP no longer recommends avoiding highly allergenic foods, unless baby is at high risk for allergy development (baby already suffers from another atopic disease, or has a sibling or parent with allergies or other atopic disease). Discuss this issue with your pediatrician if you have specific allergy concerns. If you suspect a food allergy or intolerance, stop offering the suspected food and consult with your pediatrician. If baby has trouble breathing, has swelling on the face, or develops severe vomiting or diarrhea after eating, call 911 immediately.

FOOD INTOLERANCES

Food reactions (sensitivities) are common, but most are caused by food intolerances rather than food allergies. Unlike allergies, food intolerance symptoms do not involve an immune system reaction and are instead related to the body's inability to properly digest the food. Symptoms may include gas, cramps, bloating, heartburn,

headaches, or general irritability. With a food intolerance, small amounts of the offending food may be consumed without causing symptoms, but a true food allergy will *always* trigger an immune response.

Common food intolerances include lactose intolerance, gluten intolerance, and sensitivity to food additives (including preservatives, colorings, flavorings, and sulfites). An intolerance to sulfite can even trigger asthma attacks in some people.

Many infants display food intolerances for specific foods due to their immature digestive systems, but they outgrow them between their first and second birthdays.

Digestive Health

Understanding baby's digestive health can go a long way to ensuring her overall well-being. Refer to pages 170–71 to manage the occurrence of diarrhea, constipation, or gas. Gluten sensitivity is discussed on pages 171–72.

Safe Food Preparation Practices

Before embarking on the baby food making adventure, it is important to be aware of a few food safety considerations.

Keeping Things Clean

To avoid microbial contamination and potential illness, follow a few simple steps. Be vigilant in protecting infants and children under two years, whose immune systems are still developing. Wash hands thoroughly in warm soapy water for at least twenty seconds. Use warm soapy water to keep work surfaces (cutting boards, countertops), utensils, and other cooking tools clean. For sanitizing, use the dishwasher or 1 tablespoon of unscented, chlorinated bleach in 1 gallon of water, followed by a thorough rinse. Raw meats and their juices should always remain separate from other foods. Designate separate cutting boards for produce and raw meats. Also, wash kitchen towels frequently. Rinse fresh and frozen fruits and vegetables under cold running tap water, including rind or skin that you plan to

remove, to avoid pushing contaminated dirt into the produce when cutting.

Storing Food

When you finish preparing baby food purees, store them in the freezer or refrigerator within two hours. Food stored in the freezer constantly at 0°F or below will be safe indefinitely. Although freezing prevents the growth of bacteria, it will not kill bacteria already present, so prevent potential contamination of food before freezing. Long-term freezer storage can result in freezer burn (when cold, dry freezer air pulls moisture out of food), resulting in a loss of texture and flavor, and absorption of other flavors from adjacent freezer foods. Removing as much air as possible from freezer storage bags can minimize freezer burn. The quality of most frozen puree cubes can be maintained for at least three months. Fresh or thawed baby food purees can safely be stored in the refrigerator at 40°F or below for three to five days.

Thawing Food

The safest method for thawing frozen food is in the refrigerator. Most frozen puree cubes will thaw overnight (within twelve hours) when placed in the refrigerator. For a quick-thaw approach, frozen puree cubes can also be thawed directly on the stove top in a small pot over low heat. A microwave may be used, though many studies indicate the use of microwaves may pose both potential health dangers and excessive nutrient loss from foods. If you do choose to use a microwave, consider using glass containers to avoid potential leaching of plastic chemicals into food. Also, avoid hot spots by stirring food very well after heating, and always check the temperature of heated foods before feeding to baby.

It is not advisable to thaw food at room temperature because bacteria, if present, can begin to multiply once food becomes warmer than 40°F. The "danger zone" for bacterial growth is 40°F to 140°F (5°C to 58°C), and food should not be left in this danger zone for more than two hours. Once frozen puree cubes have safely thawed, they can be stored in the refrigerator for three to five days. Do not refreeze thawed purees.

Cooking Meats

If preparing meats for baby (see page 27), ensure that all meats are thoroughly cooked because they are prone to bacterial contamination. To determine doneness, insert a food thermometer into the thickest part of the food, making sure it does not touch bone, fat, or gristle. Cook food until the thermometer reads at least 145°F for fish; 165°F for poultry; 160°F for ground beef pork, or egg dishes; and 145°F for beef, veal, or lamb steaks and roasts. Clean the thermometer with hot soapy water before and after each use.

Heating Food

If prepared baby food contains meat, fish, dairy products, or eggs, reheat the food to 165°F and then let the food cool down to a lukewarm temperature before feeding to baby. The frozen puree cubes created from the Simple Puree Recipes (chapter 3) do not contain meat, fish, dairy products, or eggs, and therefore do not need to be heated after thawing. These purees may be heated or consumed at a cool or room temperature as desired.

Leftovers

If baby has finished eating and food is left over, throw away any remaining food from the container baby was eating from. Germs from baby's mouth will be introduced into the container from the spoon, and these germs will subsequently grow in the food during storage. To avoid wasting a lot of baby food, spoon out small portions from the food container into another feeding bowl using a clean spoon. The uneaten food in the container can then be stored again in the refrigerator for later consumption.

Selection and Preparation Tips

Understanding how to optimally select and prepare whole foods is critical to successfully incorporating a wide variety of foods into a diet that baby will enjoy.

Fresh, Frozen, and Canned Foods

When shopping for whole fruits, vegetables, and legumes for preparing baby food, fresh is typically best when purchasing in-season produce, but frozen is a perfectly suitable alternative any time of year. Oftentimes frozen produce can actually have higher nutrient content than their fresh counterparts because they are harvested at peak ripeness, when nutrients are at their peak, and then immediately frozen, allowing nutrients to remain stable. Fresh produce is often harvested before peak ripeness, and therefore before nutrients have a chance to optimally develop, in order to allow for travel time and shelf time at their final destinations. Organic frozen produce is a particularly good alternative in locations where specific fresh organic produce is not available.

When using frozen produce, thaw foods completely before pureeing if they will be pureed raw (without cooking). Thawing melts any ice crystals, ensuring a smooth puree is achieved. Frozen produce that will be cooked prior to pureeing does not need to be thawed. Recipes for whole foods that are readily available for purchase as frozen are labeled with a snowflake icon ❄ in chapter 3. Quantities of many frozen fruits and vegetables needed will differ from the quantities of fresh produce indicated in the recipes of this book, because the skins/rinds and seeds of most frozen produce have already been removed. When using frozen fruits, vegetables, or legumes, one 16-ounce bag will yield approximately one freezer tray, or fifteen frozen puree cubes. Each cube is 2 tablespoons (1 fluid ounce).

Canned fruits and vegetables are not suitable for preparing homemade baby food, as many contain salt or other additives. Canned products, just like jarred baby food, are also subject to very high temperature and pressure treatments, resulting in substantial nutrient, flavor, and texture loss. An additional concern is that foods are typically packed in cans with BPA liners, which contain bisphenol-A, a controversial chemical.

The one exception for using canned foods for preparing baby food is canned beans (pinto, black, garbanzo, and so on). Canned beans are dried beans that have been previously cooked. They are nutritionally equivalent to dried beans that are cooked at home, and they take significantly less time to prepare. Many canned beans are packed with salt, however, so thoroughly rinse and drain beans before using. Use no- or low-sodium versions of beans when available. Look for "BPA-free lining" on the label.

Use Your Senses

When selecting fresh fruits and vegetables, incorporate all of your senses. Look, feel, smell, taste, and even listen (see tips on selecting melons). Avoid produce that has been damaged, is bruised, has visible mold, or has an off-odor, such as a fermented smell. One bad avocado can ruin the whole batch of puree.

When to Choose Organic

Whenever possible, purchase organic foods, especially for baby. Consuming foods that have been organically grown will significantly lower exposure to pesticides and chemical contaminants. Babies have tiny bodies and still-developing immune systems, leaving them much more susceptible than adults to potential harm. In addition to traditional supermarkets and health food stores, farmers' markets are an excellent place to find fresh, organic produce. Many small farmers may not be certified organic, but their sustainable farming practices may produce what many refer to as *beyond organic foods*. Many local farms also offer Community Supported Agriculture (CSA) programs that supply weekly produce boxes. You can also start your own garden or participate in a community garden.

When purchasing everything organic is not an option, limit your exposure to toxins. The Environmental Working Group (EWG) ranks fruits and vegetables based on their pesticide residues. EWG annually produces two lists: (1) Dirty Dozen Plus, which lists the twelve most contaminated fruits and vegetables (the "plus" category highlights crops that do not meet the traditional Dirty Dozen criteria but are highly contaminated with toxic insecticides), and (2) Clean 15, which lists the fifteen least contaminated fruits and vegetables. EWG recommends purchasing organic versions of produce featured on the Dirty Dozen Plus list, and indicates it may not be necessary to purchase organic versions of produce featured on the Clean 15 list. The current lists as of this printing are provided here. A complete list containing up-to-date rankings of additional produce can be obtained at www.ewg.org.

Recipes made from whole foods included on the Dirty Dozen Plus or Clean 15 lists are indicated in chapter 3 with a red "Dirty Dozen Plus" icon 🍎 or "Clean 15" icon ◎.

DIRTY DOZEN PLUS
(highest in pesticide residue)

Apples • Strawberries • Grapes • Celery
Peaches • Spinach • Sweet bell peppers
Nectarines (imported) • Cucumbers
Cherry tomatoes • Snap peas (imported) • Potatoes
+ Hot peppers + Kale/collard greens

CLEAN 15
(lowest in pesticide residue)

Avocados • Sweet corn • Pineapples
Cabbage • Sweet peas • Onions
Asparagus • Mangoes • Papayas • Kiwifruit
Eggplant • Grapefruit • Cantaloupe
Cauliflower • Sweet potatoes

When choosing meats and animal-derived foods (eggs, dairy), remember that the quality of the product is only as good as the quality of the animal used to make it. Standards for organically raised animals are much higher than those for conventionally raised animals, and include organic feed, no use of antibiotics or other drugs, sanitary housing conditions, freedom of movement, access to the outdoors, and conditions that accommodate the natural behavior of the animal.

Choose organic dairy products whenever possible to avoid exposure to synthetic hormones and pesticide residues that make their way into nonorganic milk. When choosing organic is not possible, choose dairy products that are free of artificial growth hormones. An artificial growth hormone commonly injected into dairy cows

simple puree recipes

Recipes in this chapter are single-ingredient recipes for creating purees of individual whole foods. You will use these purees later to build more complex meals. Your desired consistency will be different at different stages of eating. Make a very thin consistency for the beginning eater (perhaps the first time you make these purees), and a chunky texture for an advanced eater (perhaps for the second or even third time you make these purees). Texture details and considerations are discussed in depth in chapter 2. You will notice icons alongside each produce listing—these indicate whether the food is available frozen ❄, part of the Clean 15 ◎ or Dirty Dozen lists 🍎 (see page 52), or has edible skins ⊤ that will not need to be peeled after ten to twelve months of age. Each listing also includes information on the food's peak season, when it is at its best and is most widely available fresh.

Fruits

Fruits refer to the seed-containing fleshy structures of a plant that are sweet and edible in their raw state. Fruits are typically well received by babies due to their natural sweetness. When combined with certain vegetables, such as broccoli, beets, and asparagus, many fruits can dilute their strong, and sometimes objectionable, flavor profiles.

....

Pome Fruits

Pome fruits have a core of several small seeds, surrounded by a tough membrane that is encased in an edible layer of flesh. Pome fruits are members of the plant family *Rosaceae*, subfamily *pomoideae* (from which the French word for apple, *pomme*, comes). Apples and pears can both be prepared the same way.

APPLES

fall

There are more than 7,500 varieties of apples worldwide, many of which are suitable for baby. When selecting apples, avoid those that are bruised or otherwise visibly damaged. Look for apples that are firm with rich coloring, and be sure to choose varieties with low acid levels (not too tart). Suitable varieties include Golden Delicious, Red Delicious, Gala, Fuji, Jonagold, and Braeburn, to name a few. Taste it first. If it tastes sour to you, it is probably too sour for baby. Apples can be stored for several weeks in the refrigerator. Apples have a very neutral flavor profile, making them one of the most versatile foods for pairing with other purees, such as beets, parsnips, and kale (see Flavor Compatibility Guide, page 31).

PEARS

year-round (each pear variety has its own season)

There are over three thousand pear varieties worldwide, many of which are suitable for baby. A few common varieties include Bartlett, Anjou, Bosc, Comice, and Asian pears. Bartletts have the highest water content, and are easiest to puree, making them a top choice. When selecting pears, ripeness can be determined by smelling for a strong sweet aroma. Most pears soften as they ripen, but some varieties stay firm. Hold the pear gently but firmly in the palm of your hand, and use your thumb to apply slight pressure to the pear flesh located just below the stem. If the flesh yields evenly to gentle pressure, the pear is ripe and ready to eat. The higher water content of Bartletts, in particular, will lead to a soft enough fruit at peak ripeness that steaming will not be necessary before creating a puree. Pears should be stored at room temperature until ripe. If fully ripe but not yet ready to use, refrigerate pears to suppress further ripening. Like apples, pears have a relatively neutral flavor profile, allowing them to pair well with a huge variety of other purees, such as sweet peas, lentils, and green beans (see Flavor Compatibility Guide, page 31).

Apples or Pears

STEAMER RECIPE ·· MAKES 15 (2-TABLESPOON) FREEZER TRAY CUBES

1½ pounds apples
or pears (about
5 medium fruits)

Peel the fruit and cut it into 2-inch chunks, discarding the core. Place the fruit chunks in a steamer basket and set in a pot filled with 1 to 2 inches of simmering water. Cover and steam for 5 to 7 minutes, until the fruit slightly softens and can be pierced easily with a fork. Uncover and remove from heat to let the fruit cool down. Reserve the cooking liquid.

Place the fruit in a blender or food processor and puree, adding reserved cooking liquid, if necessary (probably close to ½ cup), until desired consistency is reached.

Pour the puree into a freezer tray and cover with plastic wrap or waxed paper. Place the freezer tray in the freezer for 24 hours, or until completely set, then transfer frozen cubes from the freezer tray into a labeled freezer storage bag.

Stone Fruits

Stone fruits have an outer fleshy part that surrounds a shell (stone/pit) containing a seed and include apricots, peaches, nectarines, plums, cherries (and technically almonds), as well as many hybrids. With the exception of cherries, all stone fruits can be prepared the same way. There is no need to remove the thin skins before preparing purees.

PEACHES

summer

Peaches come in two colors: white and yellow (referring to the color of the flesh inside). When selecting peaches, ripe fruit will have a flesh tender to the touch and a classic peachy aroma. Peaches will have varying colors of yellow, red, and orange in their skin (indicating variety, not ripeness), but should never have green coloring (which indicates an underripe fruit). Avoid peaches that are too firm, cracked, or bruised. Store peaches at room temperature until fully ripe. When ripe, they can be stored in the refrigerator for several additional days. Nothing beats the flavor of a ripe, juicy, summer peach all by itself, but peaches also pair well with many other flavors, such as our family favorite, raspberries (see Flavor Compatibility Guide, page 31).

NECTARINES

summer

Nectarines are a variety of peach, and similar tips apply for selecting ripe fruit. A ripe nectarine will give to gentle pressure, have slight softening on the seam side, and have a fragrant aroma. Avoid greenish nectarines, or those that are too firm, cracked, or bruised. Store nectarines at room temperature until fully ripe. When ripe, they can be stored in the refrigerator for several additional days. Nectarines pair particularly well with other summer fruits, such as cherries and berries (see Flavor Compatibility Guide, page 31).

PLUMS

summer to early fall

Plums range in color from red to purple to black, depending upon the variety. A ripe plum will yield to gentle pressure, especially at the end opposite the stem, and will have a distinct plum aroma. Avoid purchasing plums with skin damage or plums that are too firm (indicating they were harvested too early and will therefore not develop an optimally sweet flavor, even if allowed to ripen further). Plums have a relatively short season for availability, but their dried version can be found year-round (see page 81). Store plums at room temperature until fully ripe. When ripe, they can be stored in the refrigerator for several additional days. Plums pair well with many other fruits as well as green veggies like broccoli and spinach (see Flavor Compatibility Guide, page 31).

APRICOTS

early summer

The apricot is a cousin of the peach, and similar tips apply for selecting them. Ripe apricots will have a distinct, fragrant aroma. Generally, the deeper its orange color, the riper and sweeter the apricot will be. Like plums, apricots have a short season for availability, but their dried version can be found year-round (see page 81). Store apricots at room temperature until fully ripe. When ripe, they can be stored in the refrigerator for several additional days. Ripe apricots may have a slight tartness (though really ripe apricots will be supersweet with no tartness at all) that falls somewhere between a peach and a plum. These golden orange summer gems pair particularly well with other summer fruits, like berries and cherries (see Flavor Compatibility Guide, page 31).

HYBRIDS (PLUOTS, PLUMCOTS, APRIUMS, NECTARCOTS, PEACOTUMS, NECTARCOTUMS . . .)

summer

Many different stone fruit hybrids now exist and are increasingly available: pluots (75 percent plum–25 percent apricot hybrid), plumcots (50 percent plum–50 percent apricot hybrid), apriums (75 percent apricot–25 percent plum hybrid), nectarcots (nectarine-apricot hybrid), peacotums (peach-apricot-plum hybrid), nectarcotums (nectarine-apricot-plum hybrid), and more. Tips for selecting hybrid fruits and pairing them with other flavors are similar to their parent fruits. Store hybrid fruits at room temperature until fully ripe. When ripe, they can be stored in the refrigerator for several additional days.

CHERRIES

summer

Several varieties of sweet cherries exist, with the most popular in the United States being Bing, Rainier, Lambert, and Royal Ann. Sweet cherries range in color from golden-red to purple-black. The best way to know if cherries are ripe and sweet is to taste one, and you need not be shy about asking to do so when shopping. Cherries should be firm without wrinkling near the stem. The quality of cherries will quickly decline when left at room temperature; therefore, cherries should be stored in the refrigerator to maintain freshness until ready to puree. Also, avoid washing cherries until ready to puree, as moisture can be absorbed where the stem meets the fruit and lead to early spoilage. Sweet, ripe cherries have a vibrant flavor profile that pairs particularly well with summer and winter squash as well as many fruits (see Flavor Compatibility Guide, page 31).

Peaches, Nectarines, Plums, Apricots, or Hybrid Stone Fruits

NO-COOK RECIPE ·· MAKES 15 (2-TABLESPOON) FREEZER TRAY CUBES

1½ pounds stone fruit

Cut the fruit into chunks, discarding the pits. Place the fruit in a blender or food processor and puree, adding water (¼ to ½ cup) if necessary, until desired consistency is reached.

Pour the puree into a freezer tray and cover with plastic wrap or waxed paper. Place the freezer tray in the freezer for 24 hours, or until completely set, then transfer frozen cubes from the freezer tray into a labeled freezer storage bag.

Cherries

NO-COOK RECIPE ·· MAKES 15 (2-TABLESPOON) FREEZER TRAY CUBES

1 pound fresh or frozen sweet cherries

Remove stems and pit cherries, either with a cherry pitter tool (the easiest method) or by cutting cherries in half and removing pits by hand. Place cherries in a blender or food processor and puree until smooth. Additional water probably will not be needed.

Pour the puree into a freezer tray and cover with plastic wrap or waxed paper. Place the freezer tray in the freezer for 24 hours, or until completely set, then transfer frozen cubes from the freezer tray into a labeled freezer storage bag.

NOTE
Pitting fresh cherries will add time to the Amazing Make-Ahead Strategy timeline; use frozen cherries to avoid adding extra time.

Tropical and Subtropical Fruits

Tropical and subtropical fruits are grown mostly in areas with warm climates within the earth's tropical, subtropical, and Mediterranean zones. The only common characteristic shared among these fruits is their intolerance to frost.

BANANAS
winter–spring (though available year-round)

There are over one thousand varieties of bananas worldwide, but more than 95 percent of those sold in the United States are of the Cavendish variety. Ripe bananas will be yellow, with or without brown spots, and underripe bananas will be greenish. Bananas should be firm, bright, and the peel should not be crushed or cut. Other varieties of bananas can be used, but be sure to check the flavor profile before feeding to baby. Also, note that although plantains are a banana variety, they must be cooked and rarely reach the sweetness level of a Cavendish. Bananas are fragile and should be stored at room temperature until the ripening process is complete. Slow down the ripening of very ripe bananas by placing them in the refrigerator. Outer skins will continue to brown, but the inner fruit will not. Beware that refrigerating bananas irreversibly halts ripening. Bananas pair well with almost any puree (see Flavor Compatibility Guide, page 31), and work particularly well at mellowing out the flavor profiles of more strongly flavored veggies, such as broccoli and kale. Bananas can also be very easily prepared for baby by simply mashing with a fork and serving, with no processing required. However, during the initial stages of introducing solid foods, you will need to make sure there are no lumps, or baby may reject the texture. A banana is also the perfect on-the-go food.

MANGOES
spring to summer (domestic),
fall to winter (imported)

Over one thousand varieties of mangoes currently exist, any of which can be used for baby food. Ataulfo (Champagne) mangoes are supersweet and creamy (and also have a high flesh-to-seed ratio), making them an excellent choice for baby if you can find them. A ripe mango will have a full, fruity aroma emitting from the stem end, and be slightly soft to the touch. The best-flavored fruit have a yellow tinge when ripe; however, skin color may be red, yellow, green, or orange. Mangoes will continue to ripen at room temperature, but ripening will be suppressed if refrigerated. Mangoes pair very well with most fruits as well as beans (see Flavor Compatibility Guide, page 31).

KIWIFRUIT
fall to winter (domestic), spring to summer (imported)

Interestingly, kiwifruit is native to northern China and was originally known as Chinese gooseberry. When cultivation spread to New Zealand and popularity of the fruit increased, New Zealanders changed the fruit's name to match that of its national symbol, the kiwi bird, due to their shared small, brown, and furry physical characteristics. The fuzzy brown skins are entirely edible, but only when baby is a bit older, closer to the age of twelve months. When selecting kiwifruit, choose those with firm, unblemished brown skin. A ripe kiwifruit will give to slight pressure when pressed. Kiwifruit will keep for several days at room temperature and for up to one month in the refrigerator. In addition to combining very well with many fruits (see Flavor Compatibility Guide, page 31), kiwifruit pairs well with meats, as it contains an enzyme (actinidin) that helps break down protein, tenderizing meat and helping with its digestion.

PAPAYA ❄

summer to fall

There are many different types of papayas, but the most common papaya variety sold in the United States is the solo papaya from Hawaii. These papayas will have green skin that turns golden yellow when ripe. Ripe papayas will be slightly soft to the touch. Papayas will continue to ripen when stored at room temperature, but ripening will slow down if placed in the refrigerator. In addition to combining very well with most fruits (see Flavor Compatibility Guide, page 31), papayas are a great complement to meats, as they contain an enzyme (papain) that helps to break down protein, tenderizing meat and helping with its digestion.

FIGS

late spring to fall

There are several different varieties of figs. Black Mission figs are one of the sweetest varieties, making them an excellent choice for baby. Black Mission figs have dark purple skins and a light pink–colored flesh. When selecting figs, they should be very soft (but not mushy) and plump, with a rich color, unbroken skin, and stems intact. Fresh figs should have a mildly sweet aroma; if there is even the slightest fermented odor, the figs are no good. Figs do not ripen after harvesting, so be sure to choose figs that are fully ripe. Fresh figs are one of the most perishable fruits, and will usually only keep for one to two days in the refrigerator after purchasing. The dried version of figs can be readily found all year-round (see page 81). Figs pair particularly well with berries (see Flavor Compatibility Guide, page 31), as well as meats. Figs contain an enzyme (ficin) that helps break down protein, tenderizing meat and helping with its digestion.

AVOCADOS

summer (California), winter (Florida), fall (imported)

Avocados are an exceptional fruit, and I consider them to be a staple in any baby's diet. Avocados are very nutrient dense, providing healthy unsaturated fats as well as a long list of other essential nutrients. Although there are almost five hundred different varieties of avocados, Hass avocados are the most common in the United States. Hass avocados can change from a dark green to a deep purple-black color when ripe. To check for ripeness, hold the avocado in the palm of your hand. Without using fingertips (to avoid bruising), gently squeeze the avocado. If it yields to firm gentle pressure, the avocado is ripe. If the avocado does not yield to gentle pressure, it will be ripe in a couple of days. If the avocado feels mushy, it may be overripe. The skin should be tight with no visible spotting, which can indicate infection or bruising. Smell the avocados. They should not have any aroma. If they have a fermented odor, they are no good. One avocado with even slight fermentation will ruin your entire puree batch. Store avocados at room temperature until fully ripe. Fully ripe avocados can be stored in the refrigerator for up to three additional days. Along with their exceptional nutrient content, avocados have a creamy texture and a relatively neutral flavor profile, allowing for great flexibility when pairing with other purees to create a filling and nutrient-balanced meal for baby. I love to pair avocados with beans and tropical fruits like mangoes (see Flavor Compatibility Guide, page 31). Like bananas, avocados are a great on-the-go food that can be prepared by simply mashing with a fork. However, during the initial stages of introducing solid foods, you will need to make sure there are no lumps or baby may reject the texture.

Bananas

NO-COOK RECIPE | MAKES 15 (2-TABLESPOON) FREEZER TRAY CUBES

**1½ pounds
ripe bananas
(about 5 bananas)**

Peel bananas, then place banana flesh in a blender or food processor and puree until smooth. No additional water will be needed.

Pour the puree into a freezer tray and cover with plastic wrap or waxed paper. Place the freezer tray in the freezer for 24 hours, or until completely set, then transfer frozen cubes from the freezer tray into a labeled freezer storage bag.

Mangoes

NO-COOK RECIPE ·· MAKES 15 (2-TABLESPOON) FREEZER TRAY CUBES

**1½ pounds mangoes
(about 3 large
mangoes)**

Mangoes have a unique oblong flat seed at the center of the fruit that can be difficult to work around. To remove the mango seed and peel, slice off the two "cheeks" on either side of the mango pit. Then gently cut horizontal and parallel lines (forming cube shapes) into the flesh of each cheek, taking care not to cut through the skin. Use a spoon to scrape out the mango chunks, discarding the outer skin. Scrape away any remaining flesh surrounding the mango pit. Place mango flesh in a blender or food processor and puree until smooth. Additional water probably will not be needed.

Pour the puree into a freezer tray and cover with plastic wrap or waxed paper. Place the freezer tray in the freezer for 24 hours, or until completely set, then transfer frozen cubes from the freezer tray into a labeled freezer storage bag.

Kiwifruit

NO-COOK RECIPE ·· MAKES 15 (2-TABLESPOON) FREEZER TRAY CUBES

1¼ pounds kiwifruit (about 6 kiwifruit)

Cut kiwifruit in half and scoop out the flesh with a spoon, discarding the fuzzy brown skins. Seeds are edible and do not need to be removed. Place green kiwifruit flesh in a blender or food processor and puree until smooth. Additional water probably will not be needed.

Pour the puree into a freezer tray and cover with plastic wrap or waxed paper. Place the freezer tray in the freezer for 24 hours, or until completely set, then transfer frozen cubes from the freezer tray into a labeled freezer storage bag.

Papaya

NO-COOK RECIPE ·· MAKES 15 (2-TABLESPOON) FREEZER TRAY CUBES

2 pounds papayas (about 2 papayas)

Peel papaya and halve lengthwise. Use a spoon to scoop out and discard seeds from each half. Chop papaya flesh into chunks, then place in a blender or food processor and puree until smooth. Additional water probably will not be needed.

Pour the puree into a freezer tray and cover with plastic wrap or waxed paper. Place the freezer tray in the freezer for 24 hours, or until completely set, then transfer frozen cubes from the freezer tray into a labeled freezer storage bag.

Figs

NO-COOK RECIPE ·· MAKES 15 (2-TABLESPOON) FREEZER TRAY CUBES

1 pound figs

Remove stems, place figs in a blender or food processor, and puree until smooth. Additional water probably will not be needed.

Pour the puree into a freezer tray and cover with plastic wrap or waxed paper. Place the freezer tray in the freezer for 24 hours, or until completely set, then transfer frozen cubes from the freezer tray into a labeled freezer storage bag.

Avocados

NO-COOK RECIPE ·· MAKES 15 (2-TABLESPOON) FREEZER TRAY CUBES

1½ pounds avocados (about 4 avocados)

Cut avocados in half lengthwise and remove the seed. Scoop out the green and yellow avocado flesh, discarding the outer skin. Place flesh directly in a blender or food processor and puree until smooth. No additional water will be needed.

Pour the puree into a freezer tray and cover with plastic wrap or waxed paper. Place the freezer tray in the freezer for 24 hours, or until completely set, then transfer frozen cubes from the freezer tray into a labeled freezer storage bag.

Berries

Nothing screams summer like vibrantly colored, sweet berries. Berries are powerhouses of phytonutrients and their tiny seeds are all edible. All berries featured here can be prepared the same way.

BLUEBERRIES

summer

There are two main types of blueberries sold in the United States, including cultivated (highbush) and wild (lowbush), both of which are fine for baby. Ripe berries should have a deep blue color, and skins should have a white sheen called a "bloom," which is a sign of freshness. Berries should be firm, dry, and plump, with smooth skins. Check for any signs of mold, and if present, choose a different batch. Blueberries will not continue to ripen after pulling from the vine, so avoid purchasing underripe berries. Store fresh blueberries in the refrigerator and wash just before use, not ahead of time, or they will deteriorate faster. Blueberries are one of the very few "blue" foods available to incorporate into baby's rainbow of foods, and they combine well with any other fruits (see Flavor Compatibility Guide, page 31).

RASPBERRIES

midsummer to early fall

Fresh raspberries are fragile and should be purchased only one to two days prior to use. Choose berries that are plump and firm, with a vibrant red color. Avoid berries that are mushy or moldy, or those in a container with any water at the bottom, which are all signs of spoilage. Raspberries will not continue to ripen after pulling from the vine. Store fresh raspberries in the refrigerator and wash just before use, not

ahead of time, or they will deteriorate faster. Raspberries have a slightly tart, slightly floral, and almost citrusy flavor that pairs well with any other fruit as well as spinach (see Flavor Compatibility Guide, page 31). Older babies who have moved on to finger foods love a fun game of eating raspberries off of their fingertips!

BLACKBERRIES ❄

summer

Blackberries are extremely fragile and perishable. They should be purchased only one to two days prior to use. Choose berries that are plump and firm, with a vibrant black or dark purple color. Avoid berries that are mushy or moldy, or those in a container with any water at the bottom, which are all signs of spoilage. Blackberries will not continue to ripen after pulling from the vine. Store fresh blackberries in the refrigerator and wash just before use, not ahead of time, or they will deteriorate faster. Blackberries tend to be slightly less sweet than other berries, but still pair well with all fruits, especially melons (see Flavor Compatibility Guide, page 31).

STRAWBERRIES ❄

spring (California and Florida), early summer (most local strawberries in other parts of the United States)

Select strawberries that are dry with a bright, deep red color and glossy appearance, with fresh green caps. Avoid strawberries that have turned dull or bluish or have started leaking fluid. Strawberries will not continue to ripen after pulling from the vine. Store fresh strawberries in the refrigerator and wash just before use, not ahead of time, or they will deteriorate faster. Strawberries pair well with all fruits, and form a nice complement to leafy green veggies, like spinach, kale, and chard (see Flavor Compatibility Guide, page 31).

Blueberries, Raspberries, Blackberries, or Strawberries

NO-COOK RECIPE ·· MAKES 15 (2-TABLESPOON) FREEZER TRAY CUBES

1 pint (16 ounces) berries

Remove any stems. (The easiest way to remove stems from strawberries is to slide a straw in through the center from bottom to top, lifting out the entire stem and cap.) Place berries in a blender or food processor and puree until smooth. Add water, if necessary, until desired consistency is reached.

Pour the puree into a freezer tray and cover with plastic wrap or waxed paper. Place the freezer tray in the freezer for 24 hours, or until completely set, then transfer frozen cubes from the freezer tray into a labeled freezer storage bag.

NOTE
Strawberries are considered a highly acidic fruit to which some babies (though not all) may exhibit a food sensitivity. Common manifestations of sensitivity include severe diaper rash and other skin inflammation. Feel free to try strawberries, but if a sensitivity is apparent, delay reintroduction until sometime between baby's first and second birthdays.

Melons

Melons actually belong to the same gourd family as squash, but they are sweeter, juicier, and treated as fruits. Most melons have a hard outer shell, thick flesh, and a seed-filled midsection. Whole melons will typically be larger than needed to meet the recipe yields here. Refrigerate remaining melon for later. Melons have a high water content, so when serving to baby, combine melon purees with thicker foods, such as bananas or cereal purees.

WATERMELON
summer

Ripe watermelons will be firm, dense, and evenly shaped, and have a deep-pitched tone when slapped with the bottom of your palm. Avoid watermelons that are partially white or pale green (underripe) or have soft spots. Yellow color on one side is where the fruit was in contact with the ground and is not an indication of quality or ripeness. Whole watermelons store well on the kitchen counter or can be refrigerated for up to three weeks. Watermelon pairs well with other melons and berries (see Flavor Compatibility Guide, page 31). Pieces of cold watermelon also make for an excellent finger food when baby is ready, and serve as an effective relief for gums that are sore from teething.

CANTALOUPE
summer

The stem end of a ripe cantaloupe will have a fragrant, sweet, musky aroma and will be slightly soft. There should be large webbing on the skin, and a yellow or orange-tinged color. A very juicy melon will produce a sound of rattling seeds when shaken. White-yellow color on one side of the melon is where the fruit was in contact with the ground and is not an indication of quality or ripeness. Avoid melons that have green coloring or have portions of the stem remaining, indicating they were harvested too early. After harvesting, melons will continue to ripen but sugar content does not increase. Also avoid melons with soft, sunken, or dark spots. Whole cantaloupes store well on the kitchen counter or can be refrigerated for up to three weeks. Cantaloupe pairs well with many fruits, particularly other melons and berries (see Flavor Compatibility Guide, page 31).

HONEYDEW MELON
summer

Ripe honeydew melon will have a creamy yellow-colored rind and pale green flesh. Large honeydews (around 5 pounds) typically have the best flavor. Honeydews should be firm, with a slight softness at the stem end. The rattle of seeds when shaken can identify a juicy melon. Avoid melons that are too firm, too soft, blemished, or greenish. Whole melons store well on the kitchen counter or can be refrigerated for up to three weeks. Honeydew melon pairs well with other melons and berries (see Flavor Compatibility Guide, page 31).

Watermelon

NO-COOK RECIPE ·· MAKES 15 (2-TABLESPOON) FREEZER TRAY CUBES

**2½ cups
cubed seedless
watermelon flesh**

Cut watermelon in half through the center, and cut one half into sections. Remove watermelon flesh from the rind, discarding rind and adjacent white flesh. Chop 2½ cups of red watermelon fruit cubes, place in a blender or food processor, and puree until desired consistency is reached. No additional water will be needed. Note that seedless watermelons are not completely seedless, and usually contain some small white seeds. The blender or food processor can effectively grind down these edible seeds, but you may want to inspect the puree for remaining seeds and remove before freezing into puree cubes.

Pour the puree into a freezer tray and cover with plastic wrap or waxed paper. Place the freezer tray in the freezer for 24 hours, or until completely set, then transfer frozen cubes from the freezer tray into a labeled freezer storage bag.

Cantaloupe or Honeydew Melon

NO-COOK RECIPE ·· MAKES 15 (2-TABLESPOON) FREEZER TRAY CUBES

**3 cups cubed
cantaloupe or
honeydew melon
flesh (from about ½ of
a whole melon)**

Cut the melon in half, then scoop out and discard the seeds in each half. Cut each half into quarters, then run a knife between the flesh and rind to remove the rind and adjacent green layer. Chop 3 cups of melon fruit, place in a blender or food processor, and puree until smooth. No additional water will be needed.

Pour the puree into a freezer tray and cover with plastic wrap or waxed paper. Place the freezer tray in the freezer for 24 hours, or until completely set, then transfer frozen cubes from the freezer tray into a labeled freezer storage bag.

Dried Fruits

Dried fruits are simply fruits that have been dehydrated. Dried fruits are available year-round and are a wonderful option when fresh fruits are not in season. Common dried fruits that are readily available and appropriate for baby include dried plums (prunes), apricots, and figs, and all can be prepared the same way.

DRIED PLUMS (PRUNES), APRICOTS, AND FIGS

year-round

When purchasing dried fruits, select fruits with no added sugars or sulfites (which can be labeled as a variation of sulfite, bisulfite, metabisulfite, or sulfur dioxide). Sulfites are a common food preservative added to products like dried fruits, but are well known to cause food sensitivities and even allergies for some people. It is necessary to read the label of any package to ensure selection of pure, dehydrated fruit with no additives. Also, be sure to select dried fruits that have already been pitted (seeds have been removed). Dried fruits can be found prepackaged or in the bulk section of some supermarkets. Dried fruits can last for several months when stored in a dry location. Note that dried plums (prunes) are a natural laxative and should be used in moderation unless trying to alleviate constipation.

Dried Plums (Prunes), Apricots, or Figs

HEAT/STEEP RECIPE ·· MAKES 15 (2-TABLESPOON) FREEZER TRAY CUBES

2 cups water

⅓ pound dried plums, apricots, or figs (about 15)

Bring water to a simmer in a small saucepan. Add dried fruit, cover with a lid, and turn off heat. Allow dried fruit to steep for 10 minutes to rehydrate, then remove lid and allow the fruit and water to cool. Pour plumped fruit and water into a blender or food processor and puree until smooth.

Pour the puree into a freezer tray and cover with plastic wrap or waxed paper. Place the freezer tray in the freezer for 24 hours, or until completely set, then transfer frozen cubes from the freezer tray into a labeled freezer storage bag.

Vegetables

A vegetable is an edible plant or part of a plant, typically referring to the leaf, stem, root, flower, or bud, excluding seeds and sweet fruit.

....

Root Vegetables

These underground-grown veggies are particularly tasty when roasted in the oven, as the natural sugars caramelize at a high baking temperature. When chopped into small, uniform pieces, root veggies will take around 40 minutes to cook at 425°F. Steaming is a much faster method that still produces a flavorful puree. The following root vegetables—carrots, parsnips, beets, turnips, and sweet potatoes—can all be prepared the same way.

CARROTS
fall, winter, spring

Carrots can be found in a range of sizes and colors, including orange, red, yellow, white, and purple. Look for a vibrant color and smooth shape. If the greens are still attached, they should be bright green and not wilted. Slim young carrots are usually the sweetest. Baby carrots are convenient, but are typically less sweet than thin young carrots. Bagged baby carrots are usually made from full-size carrots that have been whittled down to their small size. Avoid carrots with green coloring at the stem end, cracks, blemishes, or those that are soft or rubbery. If leafy greens are attached to carrots, always remove them before storing to prevent the greens from pulling moisture out of the root. Store carrots in the refrigerator for up to three weeks. Carrots are a naturally sweet vegetable that pairs well with a large variety of other foods, including most fruits, vegetables, and legumes, making them a good complement with more strongly flavored veggies, like beets or green beans (see Flavor Compatibility Guide, page 31).

PARSNIPS
winter, early spring

Parsnips look similar to carrots, but are paler in color, and often sweeter when cooked. A rule of thumb is the whiter the flesh, the sweeter the parsnip. Choose smaller rather than larger parsnips, which tend to be woodier. As with most root vegetables, parsnips can typically be found year-round, but winter and early spring parsnips are usually the sweetest because more starches have time to turn into sugars while parsnips are frozen underground. If leafy greens are attached to parsnips, always remove them before storing to prevent the greens from pulling moisture out of the root. Store parsnips in the refrigerator for up to three weeks. Parsnips are a relatively underutilized vegetable, but these sweet root veggies are just as versatile as carrots. Parsnips pair well with a large variety of other foods, including other veggies, fruits, and legumes, and their natural sweetness can be effectively used to mellow out the stronger flavors of other veggies, like broccoli or kale (see Flavor Compatibility Guide, page 31).

BEETS

summer to fall

Beets may be found in bunches with their leafy greens still attached, or loose with no leafy greens. Beets are most often a deep garnet-red color, but can be found in a wide variety of colors, including red, golden, white, and candy cane striped (Chioggia beets). Choose small or medium-size beets, which typically have optimal flavor and tenderness. Beet skin should be firm and smooth, with a deep color. Avoid beets that have spots, bruises, or soft, wet areas, all of which indicate spoilage. Beets can be stored in the refrigerator for up to one month. If leafy greens are attached to beets, always remove them before storing to prevent the greens from pulling moisture out of the root. The leafy greens attached to beets are a highly nutritious part of the vegetable. Rather than discarding these greens, steam or sauté them for a tasty adult side dish. Beets are naturally very sweet, but they also tend to have a strong earthy flavor that many babies appreciate having diluted with a fruit like apples or pears (see Flavor Compatibility Guide, page 31). Be aware that consuming beets may cause a red color to appear in the urine and/or stools of some people, but this is not a cause for concern, as it is just undigested pigment from the beets.

TURNIPS

fall to winter

Turnips are round, similar to beets, and can range in color from white to rose to black. The most common turnips are white with a purplish crown. Choose smaller, young turnips, which are the sweetest. Turnips should be dense and firm, with no soft spots. If leafy greens are still attached, they should be bright green and not wilted.

Always remove them before storing, to prevent the greens from pulling moisture out of the root. Like beets, the leafy greens attached to turnips are a highly nutritious part of the vegetable. Rather than discarding these nutritious greens, consider steaming or sautéeing them for a tasty adult side dish. Turnips can be stored in the refrigerator for up to one month. Turnips tend to have an earthy, woody flavor that benefits from combining with sweeter flavors. Try pairing turnips with apples, pears, or carrots, along with a sprinkle of cinnamon, for a warming winter meal (see Flavor Compatibility Guide, page 31).

SWEET POTATOES

fall to winter

There are several varieties of sweet potatoes, and all can be used for baby food, but the Garnet, Jewel, and Beauregard varieties are typically the moistest. The skin color of these varieties can range from copper-orange to red to purple, with a bright to dark orange flesh. Select sweet potatoes that are firm, with no visible signs of decay. Evenly shaped potatoes are easier to cut into uniform sizes for even cooking. Do not store sweet potatoes in the refrigerator, which can produce hardening and a degraded flavor. As with any kind of potatoes, store in a cool, dry, well-ventilated container, where they can last for up to one month. Sweet potatoes, as their name implies, are very sweet when cooked, and seem to be universally loved by babies. Along with their natural sweetness, sweet potatoes have a creamy texture that pairs well with many other vegetables, legumes, and fruits. A favorite pairing for my babies was always sweet potatoes and broccoli (see Flavor Compatibility Guide, page 31).

Carrots, Parsnips, Beets, Turnips, or Sweet Potatoes

STEAMER RECIPE ·· MAKES 15 (2-TABLESPOON) FREEZER TRAY CUBES

1¼ pounds root vegetables

Peel root vegetables, then cut off and discard the ends and leafy greens, if attached. Cut vegetable flesh into ½-inch-thick slices. Place vegetable slices in a steamer basket and set in a pot filled with 1 to 2 inches of simmering water. Cover and steam for 8 to 10 minutes (carrots, parsnips) or 15 minutes (beets, turnips, sweet potatoes), until vegetables slightly soften and can be pierced easily with a fork. Uncover and remove from heat to let vegetables cool down.

Place cooked root vegetables in a blender or food processor and puree, and, if necessary, add fresh water (about ¾ cup), until desired consistency is reached.

Pour the puree into a freezer tray and cover with plastic wrap or waxed paper. Place the freezer tray in the freezer for 24 hours, or until completely set, then transfer frozen cubes from the freezer tray into a labeled freezer storage bag.

Squash

Although referred to and consumed as vegetables, squashes are actually fruits, because they contain the seeds of the plant. There are two main categories of squashes: winter squash and summer squash. Both will offer up delicious purees for baby.

WINTER SQUASH: BUTTERNUT, PUMPKIN, ACORN, DELICATA, AND BUTTERCUP ❄
early fall

Winter squash is actually a warm-weather crop, but it gets its name because it can be stored through the winter. Winter squash is harvested when mature, after the skins have significantly hardened. Winter squashes come in many sizes and shapes, but all have very thick rinds, a hollow inner cavity containing hard seeds, and very dense flesh requiring longer cooking times than summer squash. Rinds and seeds must be removed before eating. When selecting winter squash, look for those that are dense, with a firm rind, an intact stem (which helps avoid moisture loss), and dull-colored skin. Smooth, shiny skin is an indicator that the squash is not ripe. Avoid squash with bruising, cuts, or brown scarring (indicating frostbite), which can degrade quality. The hard, thick rinds of winter squashes allow them to be stored for at least one month when kept in a dry, cool location. Like root veggies, winter squashes develop a beautiful nutty flavor when roasted in the oven, but steaming is a faster method of cooking that still produces a flavorful puree. Butternut squash is the easiest of all winter squashes to prepare, because it has a thinner rind that can be peeled before cooking. Winter squashes combine well with many other veggies and legumes. They also pair particularly well with cherries (see Flavor Compatibility Guide, page 31).

SUMMER SQUASH: ZUCCHINI, CROOKNECK, STRAIGHTNECK, AND SCALLOP
midsummer to early fall

Summer squash is harvested when still immature, leaving its skin tender and edible. When selecting summer squash, look for brightly colored, shiny, unblemished skin. Make sure the squash is firm, particularly at the ends. Unlike winter squashes, there is no need to remove the thin skins or tiny seeds of these squashes before pureeing. Prepare all summer squashes the same way. Store in the refrigerator until ready to use. Summer squashes combine well with summer fruits, like nectarines and peaches, as well as a variety of vegetables and legumes (see Flavor Compatibility Guide, page 31).

Butternut Squash

1¼ pounds whole butternut squash (or 3 cups cubed squash flesh)

Peel the skin with a sharp vegetable peeler. Cut off the ends and slice the squash in half lengthwise. Scoop out and discard seeds and fibrous strings, then cut the flesh into 1-inch chunks. Place the chunks in a steamer basket and set in a pot filled with 1 to 2 inches of simmering water. Cover and steam for 7 to 10 minutes, until the squash slightly softens and can be pierced easily with a fork. Uncover and remove from heat to let the squash cool down.

Place cooked squash in a blender or food processor and puree until desired consistency is reached. Additional water probably will not be needed.

Pour the puree into a freezer tray and cover with plastic wrap or waxed paper. Place the freezer tray in the freezer for 24 hours, or until completely set, then transfer frozen cubes from the freezer tray into a labeled freezer storage bag.

Pumpkin, Acorn, Delicata, or Buttercup Squash

STEAMER RECIPE ·· MAKES 15 (2-TABLESPOON) FREEZER TRAY CUBES

**1¼ pounds whole
winter squash
(or 3 cups cubed
squash flesh)**

Carefully cut winter squash in half (a melon knife is useful for cutting through the tough rind of winter squash). Scoop out and discard the seeds and fibrous strings, then cut each half into quarters. Place quartered pieces in a steamer basket, flesh side down, and set in a pot filled with 2 inches of simmering water. Cover and steam for about 20 minutes, until the squash slightly softens and flesh can be pierced easily with a fork. Uncover and remove from heat to let squash cool down.

Scoop out squash flesh and discard rinds. Place cooked squash in a blender or food processor and puree until desired consistency is reached. Additional water probably will not be needed.

Pour the puree into a freezer tray and cover with plastic wrap or waxed paper. Place the freezer tray in the freezer for 24 hours, or until completely set, then transfer frozen cubes from the freezer tray into a labeled freezer storage bag.

Zucchini, Crookneck, Straightneck, or Scallop Squash

STEAMER RECIPE ·· MAKES 15 (2-TABLESPOON) FREEZER TRAY CUBES

1 pound summer squash

Trim off the ends and cut squash into ½-inch-thick slices. Place squash in a steamer basket and set in a pot filled with 1 to 2 inches of simmering water. Cover and steam for 5 to 7 minutes, until the squash slightly softens and can be pierced easily with a fork. Uncover and remove from heat to let the squash cool down.

Place cooked squash in a blender or food processor and puree until desired consistency is reached. Additional water probably will not be needed.

Pour the puree into a freezer tray and cover with plastic wrap or waxed paper. Place the freezer tray in the freezer for 24 hours, or until completely set, then transfer frozen cubes from the freezer tray into a labeled freezer storage bag.

Dark Leafy Greens

Dark leafy green veggies are nutritional powerhouses, providing rich sources of minerals, vitamins, and phytonutrients. Pound for pound, leafy greens are one of the most concentrated sources of nutrition of any food, making this vegetable category an important part of a well-rounded meal plan for baby.

SPINACH ❄ 🍎
spring and fall

Regular or baby spinach can be used, but baby spinach is harvested earlier than regular spinach, resulting in a smaller, more delicate and mildly flavored leaf, making it more ideal for baby food. Baby spinach, with no ribs to remove, is readily found both in bulk and prepackaged in the produce section of most supermarkets. When selecting spinach, look for a deep green, uniform color in the leaves. Avoid greens that have started to turn yellow or brown, or those that have started to wilt. Choose small to medium leaves, which have a milder flavor than larger leaves. Nutrients of spinach degrade with excessive storage time. Do not wash spinach until just before using, as excess moisture will cause leaves to wilt prematurely. Spinach should be stored in the refrigerator and consumed within three to five days. Spinach, particularly baby spinach, delivers a fairly mild flavor profile, allowing this nutrient-packed food to be mixed in with a variety other foods (see Flavor Compatibility Guide, page 31). A breakfast staple for my babies was always Green Bananas (page 119), a mixture of spinach with bananas.

KALE 🍎
winter

There are many varieties of kale, and all can be used for baby food. Lacinato kale (also called dinosaur, dino, or Tuscan kale, pictured at right) is a particularly good choice for baby, as it has a smoother texture and slightly sweeter flavor profile than other kale varieties. Kale leaves with ribs already removed can be found prepackaged in some supermarkets. When selecting kale, look for a deep green, uniform color in the leaves. Avoid greens that have started to turn yellow or brown, or those that have started to wilt. Choose small to medium leaves, which have a milder flavor than larger leaves. Nutrients of kale degrade with excessive storage time. Do not wash kale until just before using, as excess moisture will cause leaves to wilt prematurely. Kale is a hearty leafy green, and can last five to seven days when stored in the refrigerator. Kale pairs well with many foods, particularly carrots, apples, and sweet potatoes (see Flavor Compatibility Guide, page 31).

CHARD (AKA SWISS CHARD OR SILVERBEET) 🍎
summer

The leafy part of chard will always be green, but the stems (which look a lot like celery) can be white, green, yellow, red, pink, or orange. When selecting chard, look for a deep green, uniform color in the leaves. Avoid greens that have started to turn yellow or brown, or those that have started to wilt. Choose small to medium leaves, which have a milder flavor than larger leaves. Do not wash chard until just before using, as excess moisture will cause leaves to wilt prematurely. Chard has the shortest shelf life of the leafy greens. Store chard in the refrigerator for one to two days before use. Chard can be paired with a variety of foods (see Flavor Compatibility Guide, page 31). Try the yummy Sweet 'Snipped Chard recipe (page 128) that features parsnips and pears.

Spinach, Kale, or Chard

STEAMER RECIPE ·· MAKES 15 (2-TABLESPOON) FREEZER TRAY CUBES

1½ pounds leafy greens (with ribs attached), or 1 pound (16 cups) loose leafy greens (no ribs attached)

Remove large fibrous ribs (thick central stems), if attached, and discard. To remove ribs, fold leaves in half lengthwise, then tear or slice the stems out with a knife. Stack several leaves together and then coarsely chop them. Place leafy greens in a steamer basket and set in a pot filled with 1 to 2 inches of simmering water. Working in 2 or 3 batches will likely be necessary, depending upon the size of your steamer (leafy greens cook down substantially, which is why the starting quantity of leaves is so large). Cover and steam for 3 to 5 minutes, gently tossing greens to promote even cooking, until greens wilt. Remove from heat, and repeat with remaining batches, if necessary. Note that unless you use a high-speed blender (like a Vitamix), it will likely not be possible to get an ultrasmooth puree from leafy greens.

Place wilted leafy greens in a blender or food processor and puree, and, if necessary, add fresh water (about ½ cup) until desired consistency is reached.

Pour the puree into a freezer tray and cover with plastic wrap or waxed paper. Place the freezer tray in the freezer for 24 hours, or until completely set, then transfer frozen cubes from the freezer tray into a labeled freezer storage bag.

NOTE

If regular spinach is used in lieu of baby spinach, these greens will need a more thorough cleaning before use, due to the leaves collecting soil and debris when growing. The easiest way to clean large spinach leaves is to place them in a large bowl with room temperature water and stir leaves around to get debris to fall to the bottom. Rinse and repeat until no debris can be seen in the water.

Flowers and Buds

These flower heads and buds are a versatile addition to baby's meal plan. The little treelike structures of these veggies also make for convenient finger foods when baby is ready.

BROCCOLI
fall to spring

Broccoli packs a big nutrient punch, serving as a rich source of phytonutrients, minerals, and vitamins. When selecting broccoli, look for florets that are firm and compact, with an even, dark green color. Broccoli that has started to yellow or brown will have an overly strong flavor profile. It can be stored in the refrigerator for up to five days. Broccoli can have a particularly strong sulfur flavor profile that some babies may initially reject. Combine broccoli with apples, pears, or bananas to mellow out the potentially objectionable flavor (see Flavor Compatibility Guide, page 31).

CAULIFLOWER
fall

Cauliflower is a member of the cabbage family, and contains important cancer-fighting phytonutrients. When selecting cauliflower, look for a compact head with tight bud clusters and a creamy white (or vibrant orange or purple) color. A lot of green leaves surrounding the cauliflower head are good as well, as these leaves will protect the cauliflower, allowing it to last longer. Cauliflower can be stored for up to five days in the refrigerator. Cauliflower pairs well with a variety of foods, such as lentils and prunes (see Flavor Compatibility Guide, page 31).

ASPARAGUS
spring

Asparagus is *the* tender delicacy of spring. When selecting asparagus, you may choose spears that are either thick or thin, but make sure they are fresh, as asparagus loses its sweetness and becomes woody as it ages. Select asparagus spears that have tightly closed tips, and stalks that are bright green, straight, and firm. The bottom of the stalks should not be dry. Do not wash asparagus until just before use. Store asparagus as you would a flower bouquet: trim the ends of fresh spears and stand them upright in a jar filled with 1 inch of water. The jar may be stored in the refrigerator for up to two days. Asparagus combines well with foods containing milder flavors, such as summer squash (see Flavor Compatibility Guide, page 31).

Broccoli or Cauliflower

STEAMER RECIPE ·· MAKES 15 (2-TABLESPOON) FREEZER TRAY CUBES

1 pound broccoli or cauliflower florets (not including stalks)

Place the florets in a steamer basket and set in a pot filled with 1 to 2 inches of simmering water. Cover and steam for 6 to 8 minutes, until the florets slightly soften and can be pierced easily with a fork. Broccoli and colored cauliflower should maintain their original bright colors. Uncover and remove from heat to let the florets cool down.

Place the cooked florets in a blender or food processor and puree, and, if necessary, add fresh water (about ½ cup), until desired consistency is reached.

Pour the puree into a freezer tray and cover with plastic wrap or waxed paper. Place the freezer tray in the freezer for 24 hours, or until completely set, then transfer frozen cubes from the freezer tray into a labeled freezer storage bag.

Asparagus

STEAMER RECIPE ·· MAKES 15 (2-TABLESPOON) FREEZER TRAY CUBES

1½ pounds asparagus spears

Snap off and discard the woody ends of each asparagus spear (the woody part naturally breaks off at the right point when the spear is bent). Place trimmed asparagus in a steamer basket and set in a pot filled with 1 to 2 inches of simmering water. Cover and steam for 4 to 8 minutes, depending upon thickness, until the thickest part slightly softens and can be pierced easily with a fork. Uncover and remove from heat to let cool, reserving the cooking liquid.

Place the asparagus in a blender or food processor and puree, and, if necessary, add reserved cooking liquid (¼ to ½ cup), until desired consistency is reached.

Pour the puree into a freezer tray and cover with plastic wrap or waxed paper. Place the freezer tray in the freezer for 24 hours, or until completely set, then transfer frozen cubes from the freezer tray into a labeled freezer storage bag.

Legumes

Legumes are a type of vegetable pod that opens along a seam. Most legumes are considered high-protein vegetables.

....

Fresh Beans and Peas

There are two basic categories of fresh beans: (1) edible pod beans, so called because the pod that holds the beans is edible, and (2) shelled beans, which are beans that must be removed, or "shelled," from their pod before eating, because the pod is not edible. Both types of fresh beans are suitable for baby when properly prepared. Some peas also have edible pods, but infants should only consume shelled peas like sweet peas, because edible pea pods are difficult for infants to digest.

GREEN BEANS ❄
(AKA STRING BEANS OR SNAP BEANS)
late spring–fall

Green beans are edible pod beans that enjoy a long season of availability, starting late spring and lasting into the fall. When selecting fresh beans, choose those that are bright green in color, crisp, and free of blemishes. Sweeter beans will be slender (no thicker than a pencil). Do not purchase beans that have seeds visible through the pod or those that are too stiff, as these beans will be more fibrous. Store fresh green beans in the refrigerator, where they can last four to five days. Green beans combine particularly well with sweet potatoes and squash (see Flavor Compatibility Guide, page 31).

HARICOTS VERTS ❄
(AKA FRENCH GREEN BEANS OR FILET BEANS)
late spring–fall

Haricots verts (pronounced "ah-ree-koh-ver") are edible pod beans that are longer, thinner, and more delicate than regular green beans. Haricots verts may be used interchangeably with regular green beans, though their fibers are softer and their flavor is slightly more complex. When selecting haricots verts, choose fresh beans that are bright green in color, crisp, and free of blemishes. Do not purchase beans that have seeds visible through the pod or those that are too stiff, as these beans will be more fibrous. Store fresh beans in the refrigerator, where they can last four to five days.

EDAMAME ❄
(AKA IMMATURE GREEN SOYBEANS)
mid-August–September

Edamame is a highly nutritious shelled bean that offers one of the very few vegetable sources of complete protein (see page 165), making this an excellent staple in a vegetarian diet. Edamame is rarely sold fresh in the United States, as very few farms are dedicated to producing this type of soybean. If you are lucky enough to find it, fresh edamame should be used within twenty-four hours of harvesting, so it is best to purchase this legume directly from a farmer. Select edamame with green pods that have not started to yellow. Edamame is readily available frozen year-round in two forms: shelled or in pods. Since pods are inedible, save the trouble and purchase shelled frozen edamame for baby food. When baby gets older (around one and a half to two years old), it will be fun to eat edamame out of the pod as a snack. Edamame combines well with squash (see Flavor Compatibility Guide, page 31) as well as plain yogurt.

SWEET PEAS (AKA ENGLISH PEAS) ❄
early spring

Sweet peas come from a pod that is not edible, and so they must be shelled. Fresh peas have a relatively short season. Once peas have been harvested, their sugars immediately start converting into starches, so fresh peas should be used as soon as possible after purchasing for optimal sweetness. Frozen peas will actually taste better than fresh peas that have been stored too long after harvest and have subsequently become too starchy. When selecting fresh peas, choose smaller pods, which contain sweeter and more tender peas than larger pods. Select pods that are firm and green, avoiding those that are yellowing or wilting. To really know whether peas are fresh and sweet, break open a pod to look at the peas inside. Peas should be bright green, small, and firm. Once the pod is open, taste a pea or two; the pea should be tender and sweet. Store fresh peas in the refrigerator for no more than two to three days before using. Sweet peas pair particularly well with orange veggies, like carrots and sweet potatoes (see Flavor Compatibility Guide, page 31), and they also make for a great simple finger food when baby is ready to move beyond purees. Although whole edible pod peas, such as snow peas and sugar snap peas, are not appropriate for baby, they can be introduced as a nutritious snack food when baby is around one and a half to two years old.

Green Beans or Haricots Verts

STEAMER RECIPE ·· MAKES 15 (2 TABLESPOON) FREEZER TRAY CUBES

1 pound green beans or haricots verts

Trim and discard the ends of the beans. Place the beans in a steamer basket and set in a pot filled with 1 to 2 inches of simmering water. Cover and steam for about 5 minutes, until the beans, maintaining a bright green color, can be pierced easily with a fork. Uncover and remove from heat to let the beans cool down.

Place cooked beans in a blender or food processor and puree, and, if necessary, add fresh water (about ½ cup), until desired consistency is reached.

Pour the puree into a freezer tray and cover with plastic wrap or waxed paper. Place the freezer tray in the freezer for 24 hours, or until completely set, then transfer frozen cubes from the freezer tray into a labeled freezer storage bag.

Edamame

HEAT/STEEP RECIPE ·· MAKES 15 (2-TABLESPOON) FREEZER TRAY CUBES

1 pound shelled edamame

Place 5 cups water in a medium pot, cover, and bring to a simmer. Add the edamame and cook for 5 minutes. Drain the edamame, reserving cooking liquid.

Place the cooked edamame in a blender or food processor and puree, and, if necessary, add reserved cooking liquid (about ½ cup), until desired consistency is reached.

Pour the puree into a freezer tray and cover with plastic wrap or waxed paper. Place the freezer tray in the freezer for 24 hours, or until completely set, then transfer frozen cubes from the freezer tray into a labeled freezer storage bag.

Sweet Peas

2 pounds fresh sweet peas in pods, or 1 pound shelled sweet peas (fresh or frozen)

Shell peas by removing the stem end of the pod, then peel the fibrous string from the seam, open the pod, and run a thumb along the interior, scooping out the peas and discarding the pods. Place peas (fresh or frozen) in a steamer basket and set in a pot filled with 1 to 2 inches of simmering water. Cover and steam for 2 to 3 minutes, until peas turn a bright green color. Uncover and remove from heat to let the peas cool down, reserving cooking liquid.

Place cooked peas in a blender or food processor and puree, and, if necessary, add reserved cooking liquid (about ½ cup), until desired consistency is reached.

Pour the puree into a freezer tray and cover with plastic wrap or waxed paper. Place the freezer tray in the freezer for 24 hours, or until completely set, then transfer frozen cubes from the freezer tray into a labeled freezer storage bag.

NOTE
Shelling fresh sweet peas will add extra time to the Amazing Make-Ahead Strategy timeline; use frozen shelled peas to avoid adding extra time.

Option 2: Dried Beans

HEAT/STEEP RECIPE ·· MAKES 15 (2-TABLESPOON) FREEZER TRAY CUBES

1 cup dried beans
(½ pound)

1-inch strip kombu
(optional)

Before preparing, sort through the dried beans, removing any debris or beans with blemishes. Place the dried beans in a colander and rinse well under cold water.

Place beans in a large pot and cover with water to about 2 inches above the beans. Heat to a simmer and continue to simmer for 2 to 3 minutes. Remove from heat, cover, and set aside overnight.

Drain and rinse the soaked beans, then place them in a pot and cover with 2 inches of fresh water. Add the kombu. Bring the water to a boil and continue to boil gently, with the pot partially covered with a lid. (Remove lid if foaming becomes a problem.) Stir periodically and add water as needed during the cooking process to make sure the water level stays above the beans. Beans are ready when they are tender, but still hold their shape (they should mash very easily when gently squeezed with fingers). Exact cooking time depends upon many factors, including age of the beans, water hardness, altitude, and bean variety. Most of the beans listed on page 102 take from 1½ to 3 hours to cook, depending upon the factors listed above. Remove and discard the kombu strip, drain beans, and reserve cooking liquid.

Place the cooked beans in a blender or food processor and puree, and, if necessary, add reserved cooking liquid (about ½ cup), until desired consistency is reached.

Pour the puree into a freezer tray and cover with plastic wrap or waxed paper. Place the freezer tray in the freezer for 24 hours, or until completely set, then transfer frozen cubes from the freezer tray into a labeled freezer storage bag.

Lentils or Split Peas in Full Form

1½ cups water

1 cup (½ pound) dried
lentils or split peas

Bring water to a boil in a pot. Add lentils or split peas and stir. Allow the mixture to return to a boil, then reduce the heat and simmer, partially covered, for 30 to 45 minutes, until tender.

BUCKWHEAT

year-round

Buckwheat is technically a fruit seed, not a grain, but it functions as a grain when cooked. Despite its name, buckwheat does not contain wheat. Buckwheat has a uniquely triangular shape, and is available either unroasted or roasted (commonly referred to as kasha). Roasted buckwheat has a slightly nutty, earthy flavor, while the unroasted variety is rather neutral and mild. Either form of buckwheat is fine for baby. Buckwheat pairs very well with fruits, but can also be combined with any vegetable or legume purees.

MILLET

year-round

Like buckwheat, millet is actually a seed rather than a grain, but it functions as a grain when cooked. Millet has a mildly nutty, sweet flavor that combines well with any fruit, vegetable, or legume puree.

Gluten-Free Whole Grain Flour

DRY-GRIND RECIPE ·· MAKES 1 CUP (16 TABLESPOONS) FLOUR

1 cup (½ pound) gluten-free whole grains (brown rice, oats, quinoa, buckwheat, or millet)

Place gluten-free grains in a blender or food processor and grind into a fine powder. The time it takes to grind whole grains into a fine flour can range from 1 minute (Vitamix) to 5 minutes, depending upon the motor strength of the individual blender or food processor used.

Store flour in an airtight container in the refrigerator (2 to 3 months) or freezer (6 to 8 months) until ready to use for preparing whole grain cereal (see recipe, page 114).

Gluten-Free Whole Grain Cereal

HEAT/STEEP RECIPE ·· MAKES ¾ CUP (12 TABLESPOONS) COOKED CEREAL

1 cup water

2 tablespoons gluten-free whole grain flour (page 113)

In a small pot, bring water to a simmer over medium heat and slowly add the whole grain flour while whisking. Whisk continuously for 5 to 8 minutes, until all water is absorbed and the cereal is thick and smooth. Remove from heat and allow the cereal to cool.

Store in an airtight container in the refrigerator for up to 1 week.

Complete Protein Cereal (Whole Grain–Legume Cereal)

HEAT/STEEP RECIPE ·· MAKES ¾ CUP (12 TABLESPOONS) COOKED CEREAL

1 cup water

1 tablespoon whole grain flour (page 113)

1 tablespoon legume flour (page 107)

In a small pot, bring water to a simmer over medium heat and slowly add the whole grain and legume flours while whisking. Whisk continuously for 5 to 8 minutes, until all water is absorbed and the cereal is thick and smooth. Remove from heat and allow the cereal to cool.

Store in an airtight container in the refrigerator for up to 1 week.

FULL WHOLE GRAINS

WHOLE GRAIN	GRAIN-TO-WATER RATIO	BASIC COOKING METHOD
BARLEY*	1 cup : 3½ cups	Simmer 1 hour.
BROWN RICE (LONG GRAIN)	1 cup : 2 cups	Simmer 45 minutes.
BUCKWHEAT (KASHA)	1 cup : 2 cups	Simmer 20 minutes.
COUSCOUS (WHOLE WHEAT)*	1 cup : 1½ cups	Bring water to boil, add couscous, cover, and remove from heat. Let sit until water absorbs (5 to 10 minutes). Fluff with fork.
KAMUT*	1 cup : 3 cups	Soak overnight in cold water. Drain, then simmer with fresh water for 45 minutes.
MILLET	1 cup : 2½ cups	Simmer 30 minutes, remove from heat, fluff, and let sit uncovered for 20 minutes.
OATS (ROLLED)	1 cup : 2 cups	Start grain in cold water, then simmer 15 minutes.
OATS (STEEL-CUT)	1 cup : 4 cups	Start grain in cold water, then simmer 30 minutes.
OATS (WHOLE GROATS)	1 cup : 3 cups	Start grain in cold water, then simmer 1 to 1½ hours.
POLENTA	1 cup : 4 cups	Bring water to boil, add polenta in a slow stream. Constantly stir to prevent clumps, and simmer 30 minutes.
QUINOA	1 cup : 2 cups	Rinse before cooking. Simmer 20 minutes.

* Contains gluten.

•• CHAPTER 4 ••

combination puree recipes

The recipes in this section all utilize the purees from chapter 3 along with some mix-ins. Note that many purees featured here are not from the sample Amazing Whole Foods Menu (page 7), so if you followed that menu precisely, you will need to swap in some substitute purees in order to make some of these recipes (see the Flavor Compatibility Guide, page 31). The art of mixing and matching purees should be fun and flexible. Use these combination recipes as inspiration to create your own and get creative with what is in season in your area. Developing fun meal names makes the eating experience even better! When whole grains are called for, use grains in their prepared cereal form or full whole grain form, depending on baby's current texture stage (see pages 114–15).

Coconutty Mango Lassi

This recipe turns the popular mango lassi yogurt drink into an adventurous yogurt meal. Baby just may like the optional cardamom, so be sure to try it out!

1 cube Mango Puree (page 69)

⅛ teaspoon ground cardamom (optional)

1 tablespoon plain yogurt

¼ teaspoon dried coconut, finely shredded

Thaw the mango puree using your preferred thawing method (see page 50). Sprinkle on the cardamom and mix into the puree. Add the yogurt and coconut shreds, then gently stir to combine. Serve at a cool temperature.

Green Bananas

Need to get some greens into baby? Look no further than a banana cube to get the job done. This dish was a daily addition to my babies' diets. And it continues to be part of my children's diet—now in the form of green smoothies served with a straw.

1 cube Banana Puree (page 69)

1 cube Spinach Puree (page 93) or 1 cube Broccoli Puree (page 95)

Thaw purees together using your preferred thawing method (see page 50) and gently stir to combine. Serve at a cool or room temperature, or slightly warmed, as desired.

Berry Figgy Buckwheat

There is no need to even consider offering a fig cookie when you can whip up this sweet meal. Figs and raspberries complement each other fabulously, and when swirled over buckwheat you have a flavorful, fruity cereal. Hemp seed hearts can be added for extra flavor and a dose of protein and omega-3s.

1 cube Raspberry Puree
(page 77)

1 cube Fig Puree
(page 73 or 81)

1 tablespoon prepared
buckwheat cereal (page 114),
or ¼ cup whole cooked
buckwheat (page 115)

¼ teaspoon hemp seed
(optional)

Thaw the raspberry and fig purees together using your preferred thawing method (see page 50). If using prepared buckwheat cereal, mix the cereal together with the purees until thoroughly combined. If using whole cooked buckwheat, swirl the purees on top of the cooked grains and gently mix to combine. Sprinkle on hemp seed and gently mix in. Serve at a cool or room temperature, or slightly warmed, as desired.

Purple Papaya Flax Yogurt

Fruit-flavored yogurts are a versatile addition to baby's meal plan. Papaya and prunes pair surprisingly well with plain yogurt, and the addition of flaxseed provides a dose of omega-3s.

1 cube Prune Puree (page 81)

1 cube Papaya Puree (page 70)

2 tablespoons plain yogurt

¼ teaspoon ground flaxseed

Thaw the prune and papaya purees together using your preferred thawing method (see page 50). Add the yogurt and flaxseed, then gently stir to combine. Serve at a cool temperature.

Raspber-cot Quinoa

Raspberries and apricots are my two favorite fruits, so it should be no surprise that many mornings I ate this dish alongside my babies. Combined with quinoa, this sweet and tangy fruit treat turns into a filling breakfast.

1 cube Raspberry Puree
(page 77)

....

1 cube Apricot Puree
(page 65 or 81)

....

1 tablespoon prepared quinoa
cereal (page 114), or ¼ cup
whole cooked quinoa
(page 115)

Thaw the raspberry and apricot purees together using your preferred thawing method (see page 50). If using prepared quinoa cereal, mix the cereal together with the purees until thoroughly combined. If using whole cooked quinoa, swirl the raspberry and apricot purees on top of the cooked grains and gently mix to combine. Serve at a cool or room temperature, or slightly warmed, as desired.

Nutty Apple Oatmeal

Apples and cinnamon are a classic flavor pairing for oatmeal. The additional almonds in this dish provide a little more flavor depth as well as a source of protein. Feel free to increase the amount of ground almonds in this meal once baby shows an acceptance for its flavor and texture.

1 cube Apple Puree (page 61)

....

¼ teaspoon ground almonds

....

⅛ teaspoon ground cinnamon

....

1 tablespoon prepared oat
cereal (page 114), or ¼ cup
whole cooked oats
(page 115)

Thaw the apple puree using your preferred thawing method (see page 50). Add the almonds and cinnamon to the puree and thoroughly mix to combine. If using prepared oat cereal, mix the cereal together with the spiced puree until thoroughly combined. If using whole cooked oats, swirl the spiced puree on top of the cooked grains and gently mix to combine. Serve at a cool or room temperature, or slightly warmed, as desired.

Red Banana Buckwheat

Baby will love this simple combination of bananas and cherries on top of the nutty-flavored goodness of buckwheat grains.

1 cube Banana Puree (page 69)

1 cube Cherry Puree (page 65)

1 tablespoon prepared buckwheat cereal (page 114), or ¼ cup whole cooked buckwheat (page 115)

Thaw the banana and cherry purees together using your preferred thawing method (see page 50). If using prepared buckwheat cereal, mix the cereal together with the purees until thoroughly combined. If using whole cooked buckwheat, swirl the banana and cherry purees on top of the cooked grains and gently mix to combine. Serve at a cool or room temperature, or slightly warmed, as desired.

Squashed Cherry Millet

I love "squashing" recipes, and this combination is one of my favorites. Butternut squash lives up to its name, providing a creamy, buttery texture, and a nutty flavor that pairs nicely with sweet red cherries. Swirl this combination over millet to provide a hearty, warm meal.

1 cube Butternut Squash Puree (page 87)

1 cube Cherry Puree (page 65)

1 tablespoon prepared millet cereal (page 114), or ¼ cup whole cooked millet (page 115)

Thaw the butternut squash and cherry purees together using your preferred thawing method (see page 50). If using prepared millet cereal, mix the cereal together with the purees until thoroughly combined. If using whole cooked millet, swirl the purees on top of the cooked grains and gently mix to combine. Serve at a cool or room temperature, or slightly warmed, as desired.

Peachy Strawberry Salad

How many babies do you know who eat salad? Well, yours will with this recipe. The flavors and colors of this dish form a delightful combination. Be sure to verbally tell baby that this is "salad," and when you introduce an actual salad at a later stage, there will be a positive association with the name.

1 cube Peach Puree (page 65)

1 cube Strawberry Puree (page 77)

1 cube Spinach Puree (page 93)

Thaw purees together using your preferred thawing method (see page 50) and gently stir to combine. Serve at a cool or room temperature.

Spring Green Eggs and Rice

Asparagus and sweet peas are the true flavors of spring. Combine these green veggies with a smashed hard-boiled egg yolk and some brown rice to produce a well-rounded, nutrient-packed meal.

1 cube Asparagus Puree (page 95)

1 cube Sweet Pea Puree (page 100)

1 hard-boiled egg yolk (see page 153)

1 tablespoon prepared brown rice cereal (page 114), or ¼ cup whole cooked brown rice (page 115)

Thaw the asparagus and sweet pea purees together using your preferred thawing method (see page 50). Smash the hard-boiled egg yolk in a bowl with the back of a fork until slightly creamy and crumbly. Add the purees to the smashed egg yolk and mix to combine. If using prepared brown rice cereal, mix the cereal together with the purees and egg yolk until thoroughly combined. If using whole cooked brown rice, swirl the egg and puree mixture on top of the cooked grains and gently mix to combine. Serve at a cool or room temperature, or slightly warmed, as desired.

Creamy Spiced Spinach

Spinach and nutmeg are a seemingly underground flavor pairing that many complex recipes exploit. When combined with the creaminess of protein-packed cannellini beans, this simple spiced spinach becomes a filling meal.

1 cube Spinach Puree
(page 93)

....

1 cube Cannellini Bean Puree
(page 103 or 105)

....

⅛ teaspoon ground nutmeg

Thaw purees together using your preferred thawing method (see page 50). Add the nutmeg and gently stir to combine. Serve at a cool or room temperature, or slightly warmed, as desired.

Bean-go 'Cado

This is perhaps my favorite meal combination to offer to baby because it has an exceptional nutrient profile, providing beneficial fats from the avocados, protein from the black beans, and a big dose of beta-carotene and vitamin C from the mangoes. The flavors of these individual whole foods balance each other out beautifully, and the resulting creamy texture gives this tropical meal a luxurious feel.

1 cube Black Bean Puree
(page 103 or 105)

....

1 cube Mango Puree (page 69)

....

1 cube Avocado Puree
(page 73)

Thaw purees together using your preferred thawing method (see page 50) and gently stir to combine. Serve at a cool or room temperature.

Sweet Parsnips and Peas

The combination of parsnips and apples is a sweet pairing, and an extra sprinkle of cinnamon adds a warm dimension to this dish. Add this flavorful combination to split pea cereal for a more filling, protein-rich meal.

1 cube Parsnip Puree (page 85)

1 cube Apple Puree (page 61)

1 tablespoon prepared split pea cereal (107)

⅛ teaspoon cinnamon (optional)

Thaw the parnsip and apple purees together using your preferred thawing method (see page 50). Add the split pea cereal and gently mix until thoroughly combined. Sprinkle in cinnamon and stir to combine. Serve at a cool or room temperature, or slightly warmed, as desired.

Sweet 'Snipped Chard

As an adult, I love chard. But babies usually need a little help accepting the slightly bitter flavor of this nutritious leafy green, and the addition of parsnips and pears does the trick.

1 cube Chard Puree (page 93)

1 cube Parsnip Puree (page 85)

1 cube Pear Puree (page 61)

Thaw purees together using your preferred thawing method (see page 50) and gently stir to combine. Serve at a cool or room temperature, or slightly warmed, as desired.

Turned-Up Carrots and Peas

While turnips can be a difficult vegetable to love, the addition of naturally sweet carrots and peas can bring these slightly bitter veggies to a more vibrant life. Include the sage in this recipe to add another layer of complementary flavor.

1 cube Turnip Puree (page 85)

....

1 cube Carrot Puree (page 85)

....

1 cube Sweet Pea Puree (page 100)

....

⅛ teaspoon ground sage (optional)

Thaw purees together using your preferred thawing method (see page 50). Add the sage and gently stir to combine. Serve at a cool or room temperature, or slightly warmed, as desired.

Nectar-Squashed Green Beans

Nectarines and summer squash succeed well at balancing out the deep, earthy flavor of green beans. Add the nutritional yeast to this dish for a slightly savory flavor as well as an extra dose of minerals and B vitamins.

1 cube Green Bean Puree (page 99)

....

1 cube Nectarine Puree (page 65)

....

1 cube Zucchini Puree (page 89)

....

¼ teaspoon nutritional yeast (optional)

Thaw purees together using your preferred thawing method (see page 50) and gently stir to combine. Add nutritional yeast and mix in thoroughly. Serve at a cool or room temperature, or slightly warmed, as desired.

Sweet Creamy Kale

The natural sweetness of sweet potatoes effectively balances out the slight bitterness of kale, helping baby consume more of these mighty leafy greens. The creaminess and protein offered by garbanzo beans turns this dish into a satisfying meal.

1 cube Kale Puree (page 93)

1 cube Sweet Potato Puree (page 85)

1 cube Garbanzo Bean Puree (page 103 or 105)

Thaw purees together using your preferred thawing method (see page 50) and gently stir to combine. Serve at a cool or room temperature, or slightly warmed, as desired.

Curried Squashed Peas

The warmth and mild spice of curry powder contrasts beautifully with the natural sweetness of butternut squash and peas. This bold flavor combination will open up baby's appetite and encourage an adventurous palate.

1 cube Sweet Pea Puree (page 100)

1 cube Butternut Squash Puree (page 87)

⅛ teaspoon curry powder

Thaw purees together using your preferred thawing method (see page 50). Add the curry powder and gently stir to combine. Serve at a cool or room temperature, or slightly warmed, as desired.

Lentil Barley Stew

Warm baby up with this hearty combination of lentils, sweet potatoes, and barley. Kick it up a notch and mix in the turmeric.

1 cube Sweet Potato Puree (page 85)	Thaw the sweet potato puree using your preferred thawing method (see page 50). Sprinkle in the turmeric and mix to combine. Add the lentil cereal to the puree and mix until thoroughly combined. Gently fold the sweet potato and lentil mixture into the cooked barley to combine. Serve at room temperature, or slightly warmed, as desired.
⅛ teaspoon ground turmeric (optional)	
1 tablespoon prepared lentil cereal (page 107)	
¼ cup whole cooked barley (page 115)	

Nutter Butter Brocco-flower

Broccoli and cauliflower are a common pair, but the addition of peanut butter brings it to a whole new level. This filling meal can also be easily used as a veggie dip when baby is a bit older.

1 cube Broccoli Puree (page 95)	Thaw the broccoli and cauliflower purees together using your preferred thawing method (see page 50). Add the peanut butter and mix very well with a fork until thoroughly mixed in. If necessary, add water, breast milk, or formula to ensure the resulting consistency is not too thick or sticky. Serve at a cool or room temperature, or slightly warmed, as desired.
1 cube Cauliflower Puree (page 95)	
1 tablespoon peanut butter	

Minty Peas and Rice

Mint adds sophistication to a dish, and happens to pair with sweet peas particularly well. These fancy minty peas turn into a complete protein meal when combined with brown rice.

1 cube Sweet Pea Puree
(page 100)

⅛ teaspoon finely chopped
fresh mint

1 tablespoon prepared brown
rice cereal (page 114), or
¼ cup whole cooked brown rice
(page 115)

Thaw the sweet pea puree using your preferred thawing method (see page 50). Add the mint and thoroughly mix to combine. If using prepared brown rice cereal, mix the cereal together with the seasoned puree until thoroughly combined. If using whole cooked brown rice, swirl the seasoned puree on top of the cooked grains and gently mix to combine. Serve at a cool or room temperature, or slightly warmed, as desired

Cheesy Pinto Polenta

This creamy dish started off as a baby food recipe in our house, and it very quickly evolved into a full family meal. This complete protein meal will successfully satisfy and warm baby's belly—and everyone else's, too!

1 cube Pinto Bean Puree
(page 103 or 105)

1 tablespoon shredded
Cheddar cheese

¼ cup whole cooked polenta
(page 115)

Thaw the pinto bean puree in a small pot over low heat. Mix in the cheese until melted. Gently fold the cheesy pinto bean puree into the cooked polenta. Serve at room temperature, or slightly warmed, as desired.

Autumn Quinoa

The color pairing of orange sweet potatoes and black beans are a perfect symbol of fall. The addition of quinoa to this ultracreamy puree combination produces a filling, complete protein meal.

1 cube Sweet Potato Puree
(page 85)

. . . .

1 cube Black Bean Puree
(page 103 or 105)

. . . .

1 tablespoon prepared quinoa
cereal (page 114), or ¼ cup
whole cooked quinoa
(page 115)

Thaw the sweet potato and black bean purees together using your preferred thawing method (see page 50). If using prepared quinoa cereal, mix the cereal together with the purees until thoroughly combined. If using whole cooked quinoa, swirl the sweet potato and black bean purees on top of the cooked grains and gently mix to combine. Serve at a cool or room temperature, or slightly warmed, as desired.

Sea-da-mame Rice

Edamame and seaweed is a natural flavor combination inspired by Asian cuisine. Combine this complete protein puree with brown rice for a more filling meal.

1 cube Edamame Puree
(page 99)

. . . .

¼ teaspoon dried seaweed
(see page 28)

. . . .

1 tablespoon prepared brown
rice cereal (page 114), or
¼ cup whole cooked brown
rice (page 115)

Thaw the edamame puree using your preferred thawing method (see page 50). Sprinkle in the dried seaweed and gently mix into the puree. If using prepared brown rice cereal, mix the cereal together with the puree until thoroughly combined. If using whole cooked brown rice, swirl the edamame puree on top of the cooked grains and gently mix to combine. Serve at a cool or room temperature, or slightly warmed, as desired.

Rainbow Rice

This colorful, nutrient-packed rice meal will leave baby satisfied and nourished. For an even creamier rice dish, include an additional cube of Avocado Puree.

1 cube Beet Puree (page 85)

....

1 cube Avocado Puree (page 73)

....

1 cube Pear Puree (page 61)

....

1 tablespoon prepared brown rice cereal (page 114), or ¼ cup whole cooked brown rice (page 115)

Thaw the beet, avocado, and pear purees together using your preferred thawing method (see page 50). If using prepared brown rice cereal, mix the cereal together with the purees until thoroughly combined. If using whole cooked brown rice, swirl the purees on top of the cooked grains and gently mix to combine. Serve at a cool or room temperature, or slightly warmed, as desired.

Plum-Gingered Brocco-Quinoa

This dish offers up a robust combination of flavors and nutrients, and is a perfect base for introducing meat. The resulting flavor is complex and warming, and the addition of quinoa makes this a complete protein meal, with or without meat.

1 cube Broccoli Puree (page 95)

....

1 cube Plum Puree (page 65)

....

⅛ teaspoon ground ginger

....

1 tablespoon prepared quinoa cereal (page 114), or ¼ cup whole cooked quinoa (page 115)

....

1 tablespoon cooked meat (such as ground beef), finely crumbled (optional) (see page 27)

Thaw the broccoli and plum purees together using your preferred thawing method (see page 50). Add the ginger to the puree and thoroughly mix to combine. If using prepared quinoa cereal, mix the cereal together with the spiced puree until thoroughly combined. If using whole cooked quinoa, swirl the spiced puree on top of the cooked grains and gently mix to combine. Gently fold the meat into the mixture, making sure meat pieces are no larger than ¼ inch in any direction. Serve at a slightly warmed temperature if the mixture includes meat, or at a cool or room temperature for the meatless version.

Berry Kiwi Cooler

This sweet and colorful fruit combination is packed with a variety of phytonutrients, and it will effectively cool baby down on the hottest of days.

1 cube Blackberry Puree
(page 77)
....
1 cube Kiwifruit Puree
(page 70)
....
1 cube Cantaloupe Puree
(page 79)

Thaw purees together using your preferred thawing method (see page 50) and gently stir to combine. Serve at a cool or room temperature.

Blue Bango

If I ever open up a restaurant, it is going to be called the Blue Bango. This lovely fruit combination is flavorful, beautiful, and filled with a variety of nutrients and phytonutrients—everything a meal should be. Sprinkle a little wheat germ on top for an extra dose of vitamin E.

1 cube Blueberry Puree
(page 77)
....
1 cube Banana Puree (page 69)
....
1 cube Mango Puree (page 69)
....
¼ teaspoon wheat germ
(optional)

Thaw purees together using your preferred thawing method (see page 50) and gently stir to combine. Add wheat germ and mix in thoroughly. Serve at a cool or room temperature.

Pumpkin Pecan Pie

There is no reason why baby cannot enjoy pumpkin pie at the holiday meal. This simple combination of pumpkin, apples, cinnamon, and pecans will offer up a delicious, nutritious treat.

1 cube Pumpkin Puree (page 88)

1 cube Apple Puree (page 61)

¼ teaspoon ground pecans

⅛ teaspoon ground cinnamon

Thaw the pumpkin and apple purees together using your preferred thawing method (see page 50). Add the pecans and cinnamon and thoroughly mix to combine. Serve at a cool or room temperature, or slightly warmed, as desired.

Berry Tropical Melon

This refreshing fruit mélange will quench baby's hunger and thirst at the same time. A perfect cool meal on a hot summer day.

1 cube Strawberry Puree (page 77)

1 cube Kiwifruit Puree (page 70)

1 cube Watermelon Puree (page 79)

Thaw purees together using your preferred thawing method (see page 50) and gently stir to combine. Serve at a cool or room temperature.

·· CHAPTER 5 ··

finger foods and advanced meals

••

At around nine to eleven months of age, baby develops a pincer grasp (the ability to pick up objects with the thumb and forefinger), and finger foods can then be introduced to complement purees. After the pincer grasp develops, baby will soon be ready to try holding a spoon or fork—though do not expect half of what he tries to get into his mouth to make it in! It is important to let baby try to feed himself when ready to do so, but it is helpful to offer baby one spoon to work with while you use another to help feed him. Otherwise, until baby increases his coordination, the meal will end up a huge mess with little food actually being consumed. Around the age of twelve months, baby will be ready for the more advaced meals that round out this chapter.

Finger Foods

The best finger foods to offer baby are many of the same foods that you have already been offering: fresh whole foods, just not pureed. To prepare many of these simple and nutritious finger foods, just follow the same recipes given for fruit, vegetable, and legume purees in chapter 3, but eliminate the step of pureeing. Offer fresh fruits, steamed veggies, legumes, and whole grains, in addition to dairy, eggs, meats, and fish. Baby will continue eating these flavorful whole foods as long as they are consistently offered. Continue to offer purees as baby begins exploring finger foods, to be sure that baby consumes enough food to be satisfied. Follow the suggestions below to incorporate a variety of healthy finger foods into baby's diet. Since baby has a very small airway, finger foods should be cut appropriately (no longer than ¼ inch in any direction) to avoid the hazard of choking.

FRUITS Refer to recipes in chapter 3 to select and prepare optimally ripe fruits (eliminating the step of pureeing). Most fruits can be offered in the raw state, freshly cut. Apples and most pears should be steamed to soften; dried fruits are not appropriate for baby, as they may pose a choking hazard. Cut fruits no larger than ¼ inch in any direction. Small circular fruits (such as grapes, cherries, blueberries) should be halved or quartered appropriately.

VEGGIES Refer to recipes in chapter 3 to select and prepare vegetables (eliminating the step of pureeing). All vegetables should be cooked (steamed or roasted) to sufficiently soften the vegetable fibers before offering to baby. Cut cooked veggies no larger than ¼ inch in any direction.

LEGUMES Refer to recipes in chapter 3 to select and prepare legumes (eliminating the step of pureeing). All legumes should be cooked to sufficiently soften the fibers before offering to baby. Cooked dried beans should be soft enough for you to easily mash between the thumb and forefinger.

WHOLE GRAINS When baby is ready for finger foods, whole grains can be offered in new forms, including toast, crackers, and cereals. Feel free to butter the toast, or spread cream cheese or a nut butter (very thinly) on toast or crackers. Cut toast into small strips or squares for easy handling. Place a handful of O's cereal on baby's high chair tray and let him finger-feed himself while you spoon-feed a puree.

EGGS Eggs can be prepared in a variety of ways as finger foods. Always cook eggs completely through for baby. The yolk should always be firm. If you are concerned with allergies, offer baby only egg yolks, as the common egg allergen is limited to egg whites. See egg recipes in the following Advanced Meals section for preparation tips.

CHEESES Semihard cheeses can be given in the form of shreds or in small cubes, cut no larger than ¼ inch in any direction. Remember to entirely avoid raw-milk cheeses, which are made from unpasteurized milk and may contain very harmful pathogens.

MEATS AND FISH Ground, shredded, or finely diced meats are the most appropriate textures to offer baby. Meat or fish should always be thoroughly cooked (see page 27), and cut/sized appropriately to avoid choking. All cooked meat should be cut across the grain and served in pieces no larger than ¼ inch in any direction. Remove all bones and skin. Do not offer processed deli meats to baby, which are typically high in salt, nitrates, and other preservatives.

FINGER FOODS

FRESH FRUIT
Apples (steamed) • Apricots • Avocado • Bananas
Blackberries • Blueberries (halved) • Cherries (quartered)
Grapes (quartered) • Kiwifruit • Mangoes • Melons
Nectarines • Papaya • Peaches • Pears (steamed)
Plums • Raspberries • Strawberries

STEAMED VEGGIES
Asparagus • Broccoli • Butternut squash •
Carrots • Cauliflower • Parsnips • Pumpkin
Sweet potatoes • Zucchini

EGGS
Hard-boiled • Omelet • Scrambled

CHEESE
Cheddar • Colby • Colby-Jack • Edam
Emmentaler (Swiss) • Fontina • Gouda • Monterey Jack
Mozzarella • Parrano • Provolone

COOKED MEATS
Beef • Chicken • Fish • Lamb • Pork • Turkey

LEGUMES
Black beans • Green beans • Haricots verts
Navy beans • Pinto beans • Sweet peas

WHOLE GRAINS
Cereals (O's shape) • Crackers • Toast

Advanced Meals

Eventually, baby will be ready to handle the textures of everyday foods and purees will no longer be needed. By this time, baby will have already been introduced to a wide variety of whole foods and flavors, and he will have learned to not only accept but also enjoy the flavors of these foods. Baby will have developed a well-established palate that will continue accepting these same foods and flavors, only in the different forms and textures that evolve with a mature diet.

At around the age of twelve months, baby will be ready to move on to more advanced meals. This last step before completely phasing into a mature diet incorporates purees and finger foods to create meals that baby can feed himself. Beyond the initial months of starting solid foods, purees can remain a valuable ingredient when building advanced meals (for baby and adults alike!). At this advanced stage of eating, baby will be ready and eagerly attempting to put larger pieces of food into his mouth. Since you cannot chop everything into ¼-inch pieces forever, get ready to experience a little anxiety as you help baby explore the larger sizes and textures of foods that will soon become part of his mature diet. Always monitor baby while eating, and be ready to assist with choking if necessary (see page 45).

As you transition baby to a completely mature diet, just remember to keep the foods *real*. Continue offering meals made up of a wide variety of flavorful whole foods. If you can resist the urge to let processed foods sneak into baby's diet in a significant way, he will grow up to be a big kid, and eventually an adult, who continues to thrive on a healthy diet, with a true love and appreciation for the natural, beautiful flavors of whole foods. This is one of the best gifts you can ever provide for your child.

Banana Pancakes

Banana pancakes. Need I say more? Baby is going to love the introduction of baked goods with this indulgent breakfast. While you could use all whole wheat pastry flour in this recipe for maximum nutrients, the all-purpose flour adds the extra lightness and fluffiness you expect from a pancake. There is no need to top these pancakes with maple syrup, as the natural sweetness of bananas makes these sweet enough. The optional chocolate chips in this recipe will take these pancakes to the next level! Top these sweet treats with a thin layer of nut butter to make this a complete protein meal. These pancakes freeze very well, so you may want to increase the batch size and freeze some for later. Take them straight from the freezer to the toaster for a superfast and tasty meal. My babies still love to eat one of these pancakes with peanut butter as an afternoon snack.

½ cup whole wheat pastry flour

½ cup all-purpose flour

1 tablespoon granulated sugar

1½ teaspoons baking powder

¼ teaspoon salt

¾ cup plus 1 tablespoon milk (nondairy milk is a suitable alternative, if desired)

1 egg, beaten

3 (2-tablespoon) cubes Banana Puree (page 69), thawed

3 tablespoons mini chocolate chips (optional)

1 tablespoon coconut oil

In a large bowl, whisk flours, sugar, baking powder, and salt until well combined. Make a well in the flour mixture and carefully add the milk, egg, and banana puree. Stir together until just combined and all dry ingredients are completely wet. Do not overmix or the pancakes will become tough when cooked. Fold in the mini chocolate chips.

Heat a nonstick skillet over medium heat. Add coconut oil to melt. When the oil begins to sizzle, ladle ⅓ cup of the batter into the pan for each pancake. Cook until the tops of the pancakes have several bubbles and the bottoms are golden brown. Flip and cook the other side until golden brown. Transfer pancakes to a serving dish and repeat with the remaining batter.

Allow the pancakes to cool, then serve immediately. If freezing pancakes for later, layer individual pancakes between waxed paper and place them in a freezer storage bag, taking care to remove as much air as possible before sealing. Pancakes can be stored in the freezer for up to 3 months. For reheating, take individual pancakes straight from the freezer to the toaster. Toast pancakes for 1 to 2 cycles, or until warmed completely through.

MAKES 6 PANCAKES

Green Eggs and Fruit

Green eggs and ham always sounded like so much fun as a kid. I came up with this healthy spin on the children's book meal when my kids first asked if green eggs existed. Dark leafy green veggies truly make these scrambled eggs green. If you happen to have recently baked some fresh ham, feel free to add it here. Just be sure to avoid processed deli ham, which is not appropriate for baby because it is typically high in salt, nitrates, and other preservatives.

2 eggs

1 (2-tablespoon) cube Spinach Puree (page 93), thawed

1 teaspoon butter

⅓ cup diced fresh fruit

Beat the eggs together in a small bowl. Add the spinach puree and mix into the eggs to combine.

Heat a medium nonstick pan over medium-low heat. Add the butter. Once the butter melts, add the egg mixture. Allow the eggs to cook while using a wooden spoon to periodically break apart the curds of scrambled eggs. Continue cooking and breaking up the eggs until they are cooked all the way through, about 5 minutes.

Allow the eggs to cool slightly, then serve them alongside the fresh fruit.

SERVES 1 OR 2

Monkey Nutter Butter Toast

Nut butter-covered toast is one of the easiest, most filling meals you can offer your advanced eater when you are in a hurry. The addition of sliced bananas will introduce your little monkey to a flavor combination he will request for years to come. Thawed banana puree can be used if you find you do not have any fresh bananas on hand.

1 slice whole grain bread

1 tablespoon peanut butter or other nut or seed butter

½ banana, peeled and sliced into disks, or 1 (2-tablespoon) cube Banana Puree (page 69), thawed

Toast the bread. Spread the nut butter thinly on the toast and layer with banana slices or a thin layer of banana puree.

Cut the toast into small squares (one banana slice per square) and serve.

SERVES 1

Creamy Fruit Roll-Ups

Roll-ups (or wraps) are a staple lunch in our house. My kids actually call me the "Queen of Wraps." We regularly roll up bean spreads (such as hummus) with veggies, nut butters with jam or fruit, melted cheese with avocados, tuna salad with spinach, scrambled eggs with mild salsa, or hard-boiled egg slices with mayo. The versatility of a wrap is truly endless. Use baby's favorite fruits and try this sweet and creamy wrap as an introduction to the wrap world.

1 (8-inch) whole grain tortilla

2 tablespoons cream cheese

1 (2-tablespoon) fruit puree cube, thawed

Place tortilla in a dry, hot skillet and turn frequently until warmed through.

Remove the tortilla, lay it flat, and spread the cream cheese evenly to reach all edges of the tortilla. Layer with the fruit puree.

Starting at any edge, roll the tortilla tightly in one direction to create a tight spiral. Using a sharp knife (a bread knife works well here), cut the tortilla into 8 spiral "wheels." Serve immediately.

SERVES 1

Coconut Granola Parfait

Yogurt parfait is a fun, fancy spin on a simple yogurt meal. Incorporate baby's favorite fruit puree, or combination of fruit purees, to flavor this nutritious breakfast or lunch. A minimally sweetened homemade granola keeps this parfait on course for providing a tasty meal without an overload of sugar.

¼ cup plain yogurt

1 to 2 (2-tablespoon) cubes fruit puree, thawed

¼ cup coconut granola (recipe follows)

Layer all ingredients in a small bowl and gently mix to combine. Allow the granola to soften for a few minutes as it sits in the yogurt, then serve to baby.

SERVES 1

coconut granola

4 cups rolled oats

½ cup finely shredded dried coconut

¼ cup ground nuts (such as almonds or walnuts)

2 tablespoons ground flaxseed

½ cup maple syrup

1 tablespoon vanilla extract

½ teaspoon salt

Preheat oven to 275°F (135°C) and line a large baking sheet with parchment paper.

In a large bowl, combine oats, coconut, ground nuts, and flaxseed with your hands or a fork. In a separate bowl, combine maple syrup, vanilla, and salt. Add the maple syrup mixture to the oat mixture and gently combine until the dry ingredients are evenly coated with the wet ingredients. Spread the granola mixture flat and evenly on the parchment-lined baking sheet. Bake for 45 minutes.

Remove the granola from the oven and allow it to cool. Use immediately or store in an airtight container at room temperature for up to 1 week.

MAKES 5 CUPS GRANOLA

Avocado Egg Dippers

Hard-boiled eggs are one of the most convenient foods to make. It is easy enough to prepare several hard-boiled eggs at a time and store them for use later in the week. This recipe pairs a hard-boiled egg with a simple avocado sauce, which baby will enjoy dipping into.

1 (2-tablespoon) cube Avocado Puree (page 73), thawed

1 tablespoon plain yogurt

⅛ teaspoon coriander (optional)

1 hard-boiled egg (recipe follows)

Add the avocado puree, yogurt, and coriander to a small bowl and mix to thoroughly combine.

Peel the hard-boiled egg and slice it in half. Serve the hard-boiled egg halves with avocado sauce for dipping.

SERVES 1

hard-boiled eggs

3 eggs

Place eggs in a saucepan and cover with cold water by 1 inch. Bring the water to a boil over medium heat, then cover the pot and remove from heat. Let the eggs sit in the covered pan for 12 minutes. Remove the eggs one at a time with a slotted spoon and place them in a bowl of ice water to cool for 5 minutes. Peel eggs as needed when they are cool enough to handle. Store any remaining whole eggs (shells on) in the refrigerator for up to 3 days.

MAKES 3 EGGS

Gar-licky Hummus Dip

Babies and toddlers love to dip foods, and hummus is a flavorful, nutrient-filled way to allow them to do so, while also inviting the consumption of handheld veggies. This garlic-flavored hummus is so yummy that baby will be licking it from his fingers. Hummus, made from garbanzo beans and tahini, is the most popular bean dip around, but flavorful bean dips can be created with just about any beans and spices. Tahini is another name for sesame seed butter, readily found in most supermarkets. Serve with steamed veggies for dipping, like carrots, broccoli, or cauliflower (see "Finger Foods," page 143). In addition to serving as a dip, hummus is also great when spread on toast.

2 (2-tablespoon) cubes Garbanzo Bean Puree (page 103 or 105), thawed

1 tablespoon tahini

1½ teaspoons fresh lemon juice

⅛ teaspoon garlic powder

⅛ teaspoon salt

Place all ingredients in a small bowl and mix briskly with a fork to combine. Serve immediately with steamed veggies for dipping.

SERVES 1

Sweet Bean-a-dilla

This recipe is my nutrient-packed spin on the traditional quesadilla. For a less sweet version, omit the sweet potatoes and double up on the black beans. Serve this complete protein combination with a side of diced avocados for a very filling meal.

1 (2-tablespoon) cube Black Bean Puree (page 103 or 105), frozen or thawed

1 (2-tablespoon) cube Sweet Potato Puree (page 85), frozen or thawed

1 tablespoon shredded Cheddar cheese

⅛ teaspoon cumin

1 (8-inch) whole grain tortilla

Warm the black bean and sweet potato purees together in a small pot over medium heat until warmed completely through. Add cheese and cumin. Stir until cheese is melted and ingredients are thoroughly combined, then remove mixture from heat.

Place the tortilla in a dry, hot skillet and turn frequently until warmed through. Remove the tortilla, lay it flat, and spread the mixture evenly to reach all edges of the tortilla. Grab one edge of the tortilla and gently lift it to fold one half of the tortilla over the other.

Allow the bean-a-dilla to cool to an appropriate temperature for baby. Using a sharp knife, cut into bite-size squares, and serve.

SERVES 1

Broccoli Parmesan Omelet

Omelets often seem intimidating to some people, but if you can make scrambled eggs, you can make an omelet. If you have never made an omelet before, however, I recommend watching a couple of quick YouTube videos to show you how to flip one without tossing it onto the floor! Omelets are very versatile, offering unlimited possibilities of ingredient combinations that allow you to fill it with whatever you want. Some version of an omelet makes it into my family's dinner rotation almost weekly. Serve this omelet to baby with some additional finger food veggies, such as steamed asparagus.

2 eggs

1 tablespoon butter

1 (2-tablespoon) cube Broccoli Puree (page 95), thawed

1 tablespoon freshly shredded Parmesan cheese

Beat the eggs together very well in a small bowl. Heat an 8-inch nonstick pan over medium-low heat, add the butter, and let it melt. Pour in the eggs, and do not stir. Let the eggs cook until the bottom starts to set, about 1 minute. Use a heat-resistant rubber spatula to gently push one edge of the egg toward the center of the pan, then slightly tilt the pan back in the opposite direction to allow any uncooked liquid egg to flow underneath. Repeat this process around the edges of the setting omelet until there is no liquid egg left. The eggs should resemble a yellow pancake, which should slide easily around the nonstick surface of the pan. Use the spatula to loosen any stuck parts of the egg from the pan, then gently flip the omelet over to allow the other side to cook, 1 to 2 minutes.

Add the broccoli puree and spread it evenly around the top of the omelet, then sprinkle on the Parmesan cheese. Use your spatula to lift one edge of the omelet up and over to fold the omelet in half, enclosing the broccoli puree inside.

Slide the omelet out of the pan and onto a plate, allowing it to cool slightly. Using a sharp knife, cut into bite-size squares, and serve.

SERVES 1 OR 2

Squashed Mac 'n' Cheese

Mac 'n' cheese is a universal food that everyone loves. This creamy kid favorite is simple to prepare, and packs an extra nutrient punch by incorporating winter squash into the cheese sauce. Butternut squash is what we use mostly in our house, but pumpkin or any other winter squash will be just as tasty. Add some more color to this meal by serving it alongside some steamed sweet peas or broccoli. Beware: Your baby will likely forever shun the boxed variety of mac 'n' cheese when he gets used to the real thing. My kids once tasted said boxed variety and protested, "How can we eat this? This isn't even food!"

8 ounces (2 cups) dry macaroni pasta (aka elbows)

1 tablespoon olive oil

1 tablespoon butter

2 tablespoons all-purpose flour

1 cup chicken or vegetable stock

5 (2-tablespoon) cubes winter squash puree (page 87 or 88), frozen or thawed

½ cup whole milk

1¼ cups shredded sharp Cheddar cheese

¼ teaspoon ground nutmeg

½ teaspoon salt

⅛ teaspoon black pepper

Heat a pot of water to a boil for the pasta. Add the pasta and cook until al dente, following directions on the package.

While the pasta cooks, heat a pot over medium heat. Add the olive oil and butter, and allow them to melt together. Whisk in the flour and allow it to cook for 1 to 2 minutes, continuing to whisk. Whisk in the stock, then add the winter squash and stir. If the squash is frozen, continue stirring until it melts into the sauce base and is warmed through and the sauce is smooth. Stir in the milk and bring the sauce to a light boil. Lower the heat, then stir in the cheese until melted, followed by the nutmeg, salt, and pepper.

Drain the cooked pasta and combine with the cheese sauce. The pasta will look a bit "soupy" initially. Allow the pasta and sauce to cool together so the sauce can adequately thicken, approximately 15 minutes, then serve with steamed veggies. Store leftovers in the refrigerator for 3 to 5 days.

SERVES 4

Spinach Pesto Chicken Dippers

There is no need to resort to fried chicken fingers when baby can enjoy dipping strips of baked chicken into this citrusy, nutrient-packed dip. Pesto is a supersimple, flavorful sauce or dip that can be made with many different ingredient combinations, typically incorporating a leafy herb or veggie, ground nuts or seeds, olive oil, and Parmesan cheese. As an alternate meal, serve this pesto sauce tossed with cooked pasta (use 4 ounces of macaroni pasta).

1 (2-tablespoon) cube Spinach Puree (page 93), thawed

1 tablespoon ground walnuts

2 tablespoons extra-virgin olive oil

2 teaspoons fresh lemon juice

1 teaspoon grated lemon zest (use a Microplane to create fine shreds)

2 tablespoons freshly grated Parmesan (use a Microplane to create fine shreds)

⅛ teaspoon salt

2 ounces baked chicken strips (recipe follows)

Place all ingredients, except chicken, in a bowl and whisk with a fork until combined. Serve immediately with cooked chicken strips to dip.

SERVES 1

baked chicken strips

1 (4- to 6-ounce) chicken breast

1 tablespoon olive oil

Salt

Pepper

Preheat oven to 400°F (204°C). Place chicken breast on a baking pan and brush both sides with olive oil. Season lightly with salt and pepper. Bake for approximately 25 minutes, or until the internal temperature of the chicken reaches a minimum of 165°F (74°C).

Remove from the oven and allow to cool for 10 minutes. Slice across the grain into strips that baby can handle for dipping. Serve when cooled to a safe temperature for baby. Store extra in the refrigerator for 3 to 4 days.

SERVES 2 OR 3

Chocolate Macaroon Birthday Cupcakes

Birthdays are definitely a time to indulge, and this recipe does not disappoint. I love that these cupcakes store so well in the freezer, because you can ration them out more easily. The apple puree provides moistness; for a bolder flavor, try cherry puree. Instead of regular eggs, this recipe uses "flax eggs," because I prefer the springier texture that results as well as the lack of "eggy" flavor. One "flax egg" is made by simply mixing 1 tablespoon of ground flaxseed with 3 tablespoons of water. You can substitute this omega-3-rich mixture for regular eggs in almost any baked good, in a one-to-one ratio.

1½ flax eggs (1½ tablespoons ground flaxseed mixed with 4½ tablespoons water)

¾ cup whole wheat pastry flour

¾ cup all-purpose flour

1 cup finely shredded dried coconut, plus more for sprinkling

⅔ cup granulated sugar

3 tablespoons cocoa powder

1 teaspoon baking soda

¼ teaspoon salt

¼ cup coconut oil, melted

1 teaspoon vanilla extract

8 (2-tablespoon) cubes Apple Puree (page 61), thawed

CHOCOLATE GLAZE (OPTIONAL)

3 tablespoons cocoa powder

3 tablespoons granulated sugar

1 tablespoon butter

3 tablespoons water

Preheat the oven to 350°F (177°C).

Prepare the "flax eggs" by combining flaxseed and water in a small bowl and whisking with a fork. Allow the mixture to sit for 5 to 10 minutes while you work on the rest of the batter.

In a large bowl, whisk together the flours, coconut, sugar, cocoa powder, baking soda, and salt. Create a well in the center of the flour mixture and add the flax eggs, coconut oil, vanilla, and apple puree. Mix all ingredients together until just combined.

Line a cupcake pan with cupcake liners. Divide the batter to fill 12 cupcake tins. Bake for 20 minutes, or until a toothpick comes out clean when inserted in a cupcake. Remove the cupcakes from the oven and allow them to cool in the pan. While cupcakes are cooling, make the chocolate glaze.

In a medium pot over medium-high heat, whisk together the cocoa powder, sugar, butter, and water and bring to a slight boil, allowing the sauce to thicken. Remove from heat, drizzle the chocolate glaze over cooled cupcakes, and sprinkle with the additional coconut. Allow the glaze to set before serving.

To freeze cupcakes for later, first remove the cupcake liners, then place the cupcakes in a freezer storage bag lined with waxed paper, taking care to squeeze out as much air as possible before sealing. Cupcakes can be stored in the freezer for up to 3 months.

MAKES 12 CUPCAKES

APPENDIX A: ALL ABOUT HEALTH

This Appendix includes a wealth of background information on nutrients, digestive health, nitrate and mercury concerns, and special diets such as vegetarian, vegan, and gluten-free.

Nutrients

While understanding detailed information regarding specific nutrients can be helpful in creating a balanced diet, it is far more beneficial to focus on offering a wide variety of whole foods rather than meticulously calculating amounts of individual nutrients consumed (unless advised by your pediatrician to do so, due to specific health concerns). This section offers a better understanding of how food components affect general human health, as well as identifying known natural food sources of specific nutrients.

Macronutrients

Macronutrients are nutrients that our bodies need in large amounts. They are responsible for providing energy (calories).

CARBOHYDRATES

Carbohydrates are the main source of fuel for the human body, and they are the most easily digested and utilized source of energy. Carbohydrates are needed for the proper functioning of the brain, central nervous system, muscles, and kidneys. They are also important for waste elimination and maintaining intestinal health.

Simple vs. Complex

Carbohydrates are chains of sugars. Simple carbohydrates have one or two sugars in their chain, while complex carbohydrates have three or more sugars. Simple carbohydrates are generally "sweet" and are digested and absorbed relatively fast, providing quick energy. Complex carbohydrates are often referred to as "starchy" and take much longer for digestion and absorption to occur, providing a more gradual release of energy.

Simple carbohydrates, such as glucose, fructose, sucrose, and lactose, occur naturally in fruits, vegetables, and dairy products, and accompany important vitamins and minerals when eaten in their whole food form. Simple carbohydrates, in the form of added sugars, are prevalent in many processed foods, and are often referred to as "empty calories." Complex carbohydrates can be found in legumes (beans, lentils, peanuts, peas), starchy vegetables, and whole grain products.

Many refined foods, including white flour and white rice, have been stripped of many vitamins and minerals.

FIBER

Fiber is a specific type of carbohydrate found in natural plant-based foods that our bodies cannot digest. Soluble fiber absorbs water, while insoluble fiber does not. High soluble-fiber diets must be accompanied by enough water to prevent constipation. Since breast milk is largely composed of water, additional water is not typically needed in significant amounts for breast-fed infants. Insoluble fiber moves rapidly through the digestive system, speeding up the passage of food and waste in the intestinal tract, having a laxative effect. Both types of fiber are equally important for health. Natural food sources of soluble fiber include oats, legumes, nuts, seeds, fleshy fruits (apples, oranges, pears, berries, plums), and some vegetables (broccoli, carrots, sweet potatoes, and onions). Sources of insoluble fiber include whole grains, legumes, nuts, seeds, some vegetables (zucchini, celery, broccoli, cauliflower, green beans, dark leafy vegetables), many fruit and vegetable skins (sweet potatoes, white potatoes, tomatoes, kiwifruit, grapes/raisins, plums/prunes), avocados, and bananas.

PROTEIN

Proteins are an important source of energy for growth, tissue repair, and immune function as well as for making essential hormones and enzymes, and preserving lean muscle mass. Protein consumption results in increased satiety as compared to consuming carbohydrates alone, allowing the body to get full faster and stay full longer.

Proteins are made from building blocks called amino acids. There are twenty different amino acids that we consume from food, nine of which are considered essential because the human body does not make them (histidine, isoleucine, leucine, lysine, methionine, phenylalanine, threonine, tryptophan, and valine) and eleven of which are considered nonessential because the body has the ability to synthesize them (alanine, arginine, asparagine, aspartic acid, cysteine, glutamic acid, glutamine, glycine, proline, serine, and tyrosine).

Complete and Incomplete Proteins

A *complete protein* (aka high-quality protein) is a protein source that contains all nine essential amino acids. Complete proteins come from animal-based and very few vegetable sources and include meat (beef, poultry, lamb, fish), dairy products (cheeses, yogurts, kefir), eggs, soybeans (edamame), and quinoa. An *incomplete protein* (aka lower-quality protein) contains fewer then all nine essential amino acids in sufficient quantities. Most vegetable sources of protein are incomplete. However, complementary incomplete protein sources can be combined during meals, or over the course of a day, to cumulatively provide all necessary amino acids. Combine foods from any two of the following three categories of incomplete proteins to provide all essential amino acids: (1) legumes (beans, lentils, peas, peanuts), (2) whole grains, (3) nuts and seeds. Examples include brown rice and beans, or peanut butter and whole grain toast.

FAT

Fat is the most concentrated source of macronutrient energy, and it is digested more slowly than carbohydrates and proteins, resulting in increased satiety. Fat is essential for normal growth and development: it provides cushioning for organs, maintains cell membranes, and absorbs fat-soluble vitamins from foods.

Saturated, Unsaturated, and Trans Fats

There are three main types of dietary fat: saturated fat, unsaturated fat, and trans fat. Foods rich in saturated fats tend to be solid at room temperature and have a higher melting point (like butter), while foods rich in unsaturated fats tend to be liquid at room temperature and have a lower melting point (like olive oil). Human-made trans fats result from the commercial process of hydrogenation, which chemically alters unsaturated fats, changing their typical room temperature form from liquid-like to more solid-like (for example, stick margarine).

SATURATED FATS: Saturated fat is typically regarded as "bad fat," due to its links to high cholesterol, cardiovascular disease, and stroke. Naturally sourced saturated fat in moderation and as part of a balanced diet, however, can be an important supply of energy. Natural food sources of saturated fats include meats, dairy products, butter, coconut, cocoa butter, and palm kernel oil.

UNSATURATED FATS: Unsaturated fats are typically regarded as "good fats," due to their links to reduction in cardiovascular disease, improved blood sugar control, decreased blood pressure, and increased HDL ("good") cholesterol. Natural food sources of saturated fats include avocados, olives, peanuts, tree nuts (almonds, cashews, macadamia nuts, hazelnuts, pecans), seeds (pumpkin, sesame, sunflower, flaxseed, hemp, chia), soybeans, corn oil, fish, and grass-fed meats. *Essential fatty acids* are specific unsaturated fats that are not synthesized by humans but are required by the body to be healthy. There are two main classes: omega-3 and omega-6. A balance of both is necessary, though a large body of evidence suggests that increasing the relative abundance of dietary omega-3 fatty acids may have numerous health benefits, especially because the typical Western diet is omega-6 rich and omega-3 poor. Natural food sources of omega-3 fatty acids include walnuts, ground flaxseed, hemp seed, dark green leafy vegetables, seaweed, cold-water fish (including wild salmon, herring, sardines, black cod, and bluefish), grass-fed meats, and specialty eggs (typically from chickens

fed flaxseed or seaweed). Natural food sources of omega-6 fatty acids include vegetable and seed oils (corn, soybean, sunflower, safflower) and animal meats.

TRANS FATS: These are regarded as "very bad" fats, and they are still found in many processed foods, including packaged snack foods (cookies, crackers, chips), commercially baked goods, vegetable shortening, stick margarine, and fried foods.

Micronutrients

Micronutrients—vitamins and minerals—are nutrients that our bodies need in smaller amounts. Minerals help with the formation of bones and teeth, blood coagulation, muscle contraction, and balancing blood pH levels. While all vitamins—A, Bs, C, D, E, and K—are essential for the body, all minerals are not.

It is best to consume vitamins and minerals from a variety of natural food sources rather than supplements. Nutrients are generally more bioavailable (easily absorbed and assimilated by the body) when consumed from natural food sources. Additionally, many supplements may contain nutrients in excessive quantities, which could pose a health risk.

VITAMINS

Vitamins have many roles: they help release energy from foods, develop red blood cells, assist in blood clotting, and help maintain healthy eyes, skin, hair, and other organs in the body.

Fat-Soluble Vitamins: A, D, E, and K
In order for fat-soluble vitamins to be absorbed and utilized by the body, adequate dietary fat intake must occur. Fat-soluble vitamins do not need to be consumed every day because they are stored in the

liver and fatty tissues. Since fat-soluble vitamins are stored in the body for long periods of time, they can pose a risk for toxicity if consumed in excess. Eating a well-balanced diet of natural whole foods will not lead to toxicity in otherwise healthy individuals.

VITAMIN A: Vitamin A can be obtained in two main forms from foods: (1) preformed vitamin A, from animal sources such as full-fat and low-fat dairy products, animal fat, liver, fish oils, and egg yolks, and (2) beta-carotene (also called provitamin A), from plant sources such as orange-red vegetables and fruits (carrots, sweet potatoes, mangoes, apricots, cantaloupe) and dark leafy green vegetables, which the body converts into retinol (a form of vitamin A). Vitamin A is essential for normal growth, bone development, vision, reproductive health, and healthy skin. Beta-carotene, specifically, also functions as an antioxidant.

VITAMIN D: Vitamin D promotes absorption of calcium and helps maintain healthy blood levels of calcium and phosphorus, all of which are important for the development and maintenance of healthy bones and teeth. The naturally occurring form of vitamin D is known as vitamin D_3, or cholecalciferol. Vitamin D_2, found in many dietary supplements, is less effective. Natural food sources of vitamin D include egg yolks, fatty fish (salmon), liver, and fortified dairy products. When adequate sunlight (specifically, ultraviolet B radiation) is received, the human body has the ability to synthesize sufficient amounts of vitamin D (in the form of vitamin D_3) to meet nutritional needs. Adequate sunlight has been defined by some researchers as at least ten to thirty minutes of sunlight exposure to the face, arms, legs, or back without sunscreen, at least twice per week, between the hours of 10 a.m. and 3 p.m. Excessive exposure to sunlight should be limited to avoid increased risk of skin cancer.[1]

VITAMIN E: The major fat-soluble antioxidant of the body, vitamin E prevents oxidation and the propagation of free radicals. Vitamin E protects red blood cells and prevents destruction of vitamin A and vitamin C. Vitamin E also functions in cell signaling, gene expression, and regulation of other cell functions. Natural food sources of vitamin E include nuts, seeds, vegetable oils, wheat germ, dark green leafy vegetables, and avocados.

VITAMIN K: This vitamin is necessary in the body for normal blood clotting and for synthesis of proteins found in bones, kidneys, and blood. Vitamin K_1 (phylloquinone) is found in plants, and vitamin K_2 (menaquinone) is found in much smaller quantities from animal sources. Intestinal bacteria actually synthesize a significant portion of the vitamin K requirements for the human body. One reason why newborns are given a vitamin K injection shortly after birth is to give them a short-term supply of the vitamin until their intestines become colonized with enough bacteria to produce it for themselves. Prolonged use of antibiotics can lead to vitamin K deficiency because antibiotics destroy the vitamin K–producing bacteria. Natural food sources of vitamin K include dark green leafy vegetables (kale, spinach, chard, parsley), broccoli, brussels sprouts, asparagus, peas, cashew nuts, pistachios, and pumpkin seeds.

1. M. F. Holick, "Vitamin D Deficiency," *New England Journal of Medicine* 357 (2007): 266–81; M. F. Holick, "Vitamin D: The Underappreciated D-lightful Hormone That Is Important for Skeletal and Cellular Health," *Current Opinion in Endocrinology, Diabetes, and Obesity* 9 (2002): 87–98; Institute of Medicine/Food and Nutrition Board, *Dietary Reference Intakes for Calcium and Vitamin D.* Washington, DC: National Academy Press, 2010.

Water-Soluble Vitamins (Bs and C)

Unlike fat-soluble vitamins, water-soluble vitamins are not stored in the body, and therefore need to be regularly consumed. Excess will be readily excreted in the urine and are much less likely to pose a risk of toxicity.

VITAMIN Bs: Vitamin Bs include a total of eight B vitamins, all of which play important, unique roles in cell metabolism. B vitamins include B_1 (thiamin), B_2 (riboflavin), B_3 (niacin), B_5 (pantothenic acid), B_6 (pyridoxine), B_7 (biotin), B_9 (folic acid), and B_{12} (cobalamin). B vitamins are fairly ubiquitous throughout the categories of whole foods, including whole grains, legumes, nuts, seeds, vegetables, fruits, meats, fish, dairy, eggs, molasses, and nutritional yeast. Vitamin B_{12} is naturally found only in animal products (meats, fish, dairy, eggs), making vitamin B_{12} deficiency a major concern with vegan diets, but can also be consumed through fortified foods, including nutritional yeast. (However, fortified sources are typically not as bioavailable as B_{12} consumed from animal products.)

VITAMIN C: Vitamin C is needed for the formation of collagen, a protein used to make skin, tendons, ligaments, and blood vessels. It helps to heal wounds and form scar tissue; repair and maintain cartilage, bones, and teeth; and boost the immune system. Vitamin C also functions as a major antioxidant. Natural food sources of vitamin C include citrus fruits, strawberries, kiwifruit, mangoes, papaya, cantaloupe, pineapple, red and green sweet bell peppers, tomatoes, leafy greens (spinach, kale, chard), brussels sprouts, broccoli, cauliflower, and turnips.

MINERALS

While all vitamins are essential for the human body, all minerals are not. Some important minerals to monitor in the diet, specifically in the diet of baby, include iron and calcium. Other essential minerals not discussed here include sodium, magnesium, potassium, iodine, selenium, zinc, and phosphorus.

Iron

Iron functions primarily as a carrier of oxygen in the body. Infants are born with a natural supply of iron stored in their bodies. After six months, these iron stores are typically depleted and baby must consume iron from external food sources. Iron deficiency symptoms including paleness and a general feeling of weakness and fatigue. Iron is naturally available from both animal- and plant-based foods, referred to as heme iron and nonheme iron, respectively. Heme iron is only found in meats (particularly dark), including beef, poultry, pork, lamb, and fish, and is much more readily absorbed than nonheme iron from plant sources, such as beans, lentils, spinach, nuts, seeds, dried fruits (apricots, prunes, dates, raisins), soybeans, and blackstrap molasses. Vegetarians should note that when relying on nonheme sources for iron, pairing the iron source with a vitamin C–rich food will greatly enhance iron absorption when consumed together at the same meal. Conversely, pairing a nonheme iron source with a calcium-rich food (such as dairy products) at the same meal will inhibit iron absorption.

Calcium

Calcium functions to build bones and teeth, and is also needed for muscle, heart, and digestive health. Breast milk or formula typically provides all of the calcium that baby needs. When breast milk or formula consumption significantly declines, usually by baby's first birthday, food sources of calcium should be included in baby's diet, such as dairy products, eggs, nuts, seeds (especially sesame), dark green leafy vegetables, soybeans, and seaweed.

NUTRIENTS AND DIETARY SOURCES

	FRUITS	VEGETABLES	LEGUMES	WHOLE GRAINS	NUTS	SEEDS	EGGS	DAIRY	FISH	MEAT
PHYTONUTRIENTS	•	•	•	•	•	•				
SIMPLE CARBOHYDRATES	•	•						•		
COMPLEX CARBOHYDRATES		•	•	•	•	•				
FIBER	•	•	•	•	•	•				
COMPLETE PROTEIN			• (Edamame)	• (Quinoa)			•	•	•	•
INCOMPLETE PROTEIN						•				
UNSATURATED FAT	• (Avocado)				•	•		•	•	•
OMEGA-3 FAT (SPECIFIC TYPE OF UNSATURATED FAT)		• (Leafy greens)			•		• (Specialty)		• (Cold-water)	• (Grass-fed)
SATURATED FAT							•	•		•
VITAMIN A	•	•					•	•		
VITAMIN D							•	• (Fortified)	•	•
VITAMIN E	• (Avocado)				•	•				
VITAMIN K		•	•		•	•				
VITAMIN Bs	•	•	•	•	•	•			•	•
VITAMIN B12							•	•	•	•
VITAMIN C	• (Especially berries, cantaloupe, citrus, kiwifruit, mangoes, papaya)	• (Especially broccoli, cauliflower, leafy greens, turnips)								
HEME IRON									•	•
NONHEME IRON	• (Dried fruits, especially apricots)	• (Asparagus, leafy greens, potatoes with skins)	•	• (Barley, quinoa, wheat)	•	• (Especially sesame [tahini])	•			
CALCIUM	• (Dried fruits)	• (Broccoli, leafy greens)	• (Edamame, garbanzo beans)		•	• (Especially sesame [tahini])	•	•	•	

This chart was compiled through analyzing data of individual whole foods using the USDA National Nutrient Database. Nutrients primarily found only in specific foods within a food category are indicated.

Digestive Health

Understanding baby's digestive health can go a long way to ensuring her overall well-being.

Diarrhea

There are many potential causes for diarrhea in infants and young children. Always seek the advice of a pediatrician for treatment. A commonly recommended dietary treatment for diarrhea is the BRAT diet (Bananas, Rice, Applesauce, and Toast) to help firm up loose stools.

A specific treatment for diarrhea to consider is probiotics. Probiotics are "good" bacteria that naturally reside in the intestines and play an active role in maintaining digestive health. If a bacterial infection (from "bad" bacteria) is or was present, consuming probiotics can help restore balance and effectively relieve diarrhea. It is also helpful to give probiotics following treatment with antibiotics, which inadvertently destroy the "good" bacteria while combating the "bad." Foods labeled as containing "live and active cultures," such as many yogurts, already contain probiotics. Probiotics can also be purchased as a dietary supplement (typically as a powdered capsule), and may be safely mixed with baby's food. I personally keep a constant supply of probiotics on hand for immediate use when digestive distress occurs for anyone in the family, including the dog!

Constipation

One of the most common causes of constipation in infants is the introduction of solid foods, as the digestive system takes time to learn how to process and absorb new nutrients. To help relieve constipation, reverse the BRAT diet, and avoid bananas, rice, applesauce, and toast. Foods that act as natural laxatives include dried plums (prunes), mangoes, pears, and apricots. Other techniques to help relieve constipation include giving baby a gentle tummy massage and moving her legs as if riding a bicycle to promote digestive movement.

Gas

Gas is typically caused by either swallowed air (which can occur during a long duration of crying) or from the normal breakdown of undigested foods. Foods that make their way to the large intestine undigested can be feasted upon by the friendly bacteria that live there. The result is often gas.

Some foods, such as beans and cruciferous vegetables (like broccoli and cabbage), contain oligosaccharides, which are a form of fiber that the human body lacks the enzymes to digest. When consumed, this fiber makes its way to the large intestine undigested, and specific bacteria that reside there digest it for you, which may produce gas. Do not assume that baby will have a difficult time digesting foods commonly known to produce gas. The types and quantities of intestinal bacteria vary among people. Additionally, many people will notice digestive improvement (decreased gas) when these foods are gradually introduced into the diet over a long period of time.

Do not fear potentially gas-producing foods. Many of these foods are loaded with nutritional benefits. Gas is an entirely normal part of digestion and should really only be considered an issue if causing physical discomfort. If baby seems only slightly and temporarily uncomfortable when passing gas, there should be no cause for concern. However, if baby is noticeably uncomfortable, often turning red and crying while trying to pass gas, avoid known gas-producing foods (though they should be intermittently reintroduced later to offer the digestive system an opportunity to adapt).

There are ways to reduce the occurrence of gas when consuming known gas-producing foods. Always introduce known gas-producing foods gradually. Soak and rinse beans before cooking to allow many of the water-soluble oligosaccharides to come out and be washed away. Cooking beans with kombu, a sea vegetable, is also known to improve their digestion by breaking down oligosaccharides during cooking (see page 105).

Vegetarian, Vegan, and Gluten-Free Diets

Feeding vegetarian, vegan, and gluten-free diets to infants and toddlers can be a healthy lifestyle choice, if all essential nutrients for proper growth are obtained.

Vegetarian and Vegan

Vegetarian diets are plant based diets that eliminate meat, and may also restrict or eliminate a range of foods derived from animals. There are various vegetarian diet styles, including lacto-ovo vegetarian diets, which include dairy and eggs, and vegan diets, which omit all animal-derived products.

It is relatively easy to obtain an adequate supply of nutrients from a well-balanced lacto-ovo vegetarian diet. It can be significantly more challenging, however, to ensure that an adequate supply of essential nutrients is obtained through a vegan diet. Vegetarians should consume an adequate amount of all essential amino acids by eating a wide variety of protein sources. Certain vegetable proteins can be combined to yield a complete supply of amino acids (see page 165). Vegetarian diets should also include adequate sources of iron, to avoid iron deficiency anemia. Plant sources of iron are not as readily absorbed as animal sources, but consuming plant-based iron with a vitamin C–rich food will enhance its absorption (see page 168). Vitamin B_{12} is one essential nutrient that is found naturally only in animal-derived foods, making this a major concern for vegans. Vegans can consume vitamin B_{12} through fortified foods; however, fortified sources are typically not as bioavailable (easily assimilated by the body). Vegan diets, especially for infants and young children, should be decided with great caution, and only with proper education and planning. Refer to "Vitamin Bs," page 168, and the nutrient chart on page 169 for helpful nutrient information.

Gluten-Free

A gluten-free diet excludes the protein gluten, which is found in several grains such as barley, rye, triticale, and wheat (including bulgur, durum, farina, graham, kamut, semolina, and spelt). Although oats do not naturally contain gluten, they can be contaminated with wheat during growing and processing unless they are certified gluten-free. A gluten-free diet is used to treat a spectrum of gluten-intolerance disorders, ranging from mild gluten sensitivity to celiac disease. For some people, removing gluten from the diet can alleviate a variety of ailments and result in improved overall health.

Any form of gluten intolerance can cause dramatic intestinal distress (stomachaches, gas, diarrhea) and trigger additional health problems, including headaches, fatigue, joint or muscle pain, skin rashes, or acne. Celiac disease (the most severe form) can be diagnosed by a physician, but milder forms of gluten sensitivity can only be diagnosed by default.

It is entirely safe to offer a gluten-free diet to baby. Gluten-free grains are actually recommended until around the age of ten months, because gluten can be difficult for babies to digest. See the recipe for Gluten-free Whole Grain Cereal on page 114. Gluten-free grains, starches, and flours include amaranth, arrowroot, bean flours, corn (polenta), flax meal, millet oats (if certified gluten-free), potato flour, quinoa, rice, sorghum, soy, tapioca, teff, and buckweat (do not let the name confuse you; buckwheat does not contain wheat). Also, the majority of whole foods are gluten-free, including fruits, vegetables, legumes, nuts, seeds, eggs, meat, fish, and most dairy products. Many processed foods, on the other hand, often contain gluten, including most breads, crackers, pastas, cereals, bakery goods, fried foods, sauces, and dressings. Keep in mind that gluten-free versions of these foods are not necessarily healthier options beyond not containing gluten.

Nitrates

Nitrates are a natural component of plants and nitrate-containing fertilizers that aid in the growth of fruits and vegetables. Vegetables contain varying levels of nitrates depending upon many factors, including vegetable type, the environment they are grown in, and how they are stored and processed. In addition to being present in some vegetables, nitrates often seep into well water.

When nitrates are digested, they can be particularly harmful to infants younger than six months of age. Infants have an insufficient level of stomach acid, which allows the rapid conversion of nitrates into nitrites. Nitrites react with hemoglobin in the blood, forming high amounts of methemoglobin, which can lead to oxygen deprivation to the blood and vital organs. This can result in nitrate poisoning, or "blue baby syndrome" (methemoglobinemia), which can be fatal.

Nitrate poisoning is rare and usually related to the use of contaminated well water to prepare infant formula rather than the consumption of nitrate-containing vegetables. Nonetheless, do not feed high-nitrate-containing vegetables (see page 40) to infants under six months of age. Nitrate-containing vegetables should not be feared after the age of six months, since baby will then have enough stomach acidity to prevent the conversion of nitrates into nitrites.

Use the following tips to limit nitrate exposure:

- If you use well water, have it tested for nitrate-nitrogen content (maximum level should be less than 10 ppm [or 10 mg/L]). If well water exceeds this limit, do not use it to make homemade baby food or formula, or offer it to baby it any form. Use bottled water instead.

- Avoid offering high-nitrate-containing vegetables until six months of age.

- Limit storage time of nitrate-containing vegetables prior to pureeing and freezing, as nitrates continue to develop during storage (though not in the freezer).

- When preparing baby purees with high-nitrate produce, do not use cooking liquid reserved from steaming to thin out the puree.

- Choose organic. Organically grown produce has fewer nitrates than conventionally grown produce due to lack of fertilizer use.

Mercury and Fish

Fish and shellfish provide an excellent source of nutrients, including protein and omega-3 fatty acids. Some fish, however, contain unsafe levels of methylmercury, a form of mercury that can be toxic when consumed at high levels. Nearly all fish and shellfish contain traces of mercury, but some contain high enough amounts to harm an unborn baby or young child's developing nervous system. In 2004, the Environmental Protection Agency (EPA) and Food and Drug Administration (FDA) issued a standing joint federal advisory for mercury in fish, advising women who may become pregnant, pregnant women, nursing mothers, and young children to avoid high-mercury-containing fish.

Mercury occurs naturally in the environment and is also released into the air from industrial pollution. Most mercury pollution in the air then falls directly into waterways or onto land, where it can be washed into bodies of water. Bacteria in water can change mercury into methylmercury, which is absorbed by small organisms in the water. When fish feed on these organisms, methylmercury quickly builds up in their muscle tissue. Since big fish feed on smaller fish, methylmercury is particularly high in their muscle tissue. The health benefits of eating fish can and should be enjoyed by choosing fish and shellfish with low mercury levels, while avoiding consumption of high-mercury-containing fish (see page 41).

APPENDIX B: TOOLS AND CONVERSION CHARTS

Tools

Here is an annotated list of all the tools you'll need for the Amazing Make-Ahead Strategy.

BABY SPOON: Needed for feeding baby.

BLENDER OR FOOD PROCESSOR: Most blenders and food processors will get the job done. High-speed blenders, however, have a much more powerful motor and can produce an ultrasmooth puree like no other machine can. I highly recommend the Vitamix, which is solid, powerful, reliable, and durable. In addition to producing ultrasmooth purees, the Vitamix can produce perfectly ground grains for baby cereals, and can handle tough jobs, such as creating nut butters. This machine is rather expensive, but it is one of the best kitchen investments you can make.

COLANDER: Needed for rinsing and draining whole foods.

CUTTING BOARD: Needed for cutting and preparing whole foods.

FREEZER STORAGE BAGS (1-QUART SIZE): Used for storing frozen baby food puree cubes. Use freezer storage bags, not regular plastic storage bags. Freezer storage bags are made with thicker plastic, prevent moisture loss and freezer burn, and allow longer storage time.

FREEZER STORAGE BASKET (11¾ x 7½ x 12½): Used for organizing and storing all bags of baby food puree cubes in the freezer (see photo on page 23).

FREEZER TRAYS: Used for freezing baby food purees into cubes. Although any ice cube trays can be used, my favorite freezer trays are those shown on page 11. These trays are made of silicone and each holds fifteen cubes, 2 tablespoons (1 fluid ounce) per cube. These trays are perfect for making baby food for several reasons: (1) they produce perfect cube shapes, which (other than being cute) accommodate very compact, neatly organized storage in freezer bags; (2) the flexible silicone material allows the frozen puree cubes to dislodge very easily; (3) silicone is a food-safe material, with no BPAs or other plastic chemicals to worry about; (4) the trays have a lip around the edge, allowing them to be stacked in the freezer without spilling; (5) they are compact, taking up minimal freezer space; (6) recipes in this book have been written to produce quantities to fill one of these trays. A total of six of these trays, or their equivalent, will be needed to use the Amazing Make-Ahead Strategy. You can find these trays, along with the freezer basket and other supplies needed for this process, at www.AmazingBabyFood.com or specialty kitchen supply shops.

GLOVES: Gloves protect your hands from cold when transferring frozen baby food puree cubes into freezer storage bags. Wear a thin insulating glove to protect hands from the cold with disposable gloves (approved for food handling) on top to protect them from getting wet and soiled.

KNIFE: Needed for cutting whole foods. Use any well-sharpened knife.

PLASTIC WRAP OR WAXED PAPER: Used for covering freezer trays during the freezing process. If you are concerned about BPAs from plastic wrap touching puree cubes, waxed paper is a suitable alternative. Waxed paper can also be used to line freezer storage bags to prevent frozen puree cubes from coming into contact with the plastic material.

POT (SMALL) WITH LID: Needed for "heat/steep" recipes in this book.

PREP BOWLS: Used for holding and separating individual foods during the cooking and preparation process. A total of six will be needed for the Amazing Make-Ahead Strategy.

RUBBER SPATULA: Used for scraping out purees from the blender.

STEAMER: Essential for preparing baby food using the "steamer" recipes in this book. There are many different types of steamers to choose from. Only one steamer basket is necessary, but multiple steamers are more efficient. Whichever steamer you choose, the diameter of the basket should be at least 11 inches to accommodate the recipe sizes in this book.

STORAGE CONTAINERS WITH LIDS: Used for a variety of purposes, including thawing frozen baby food cubes in the refrigerator, taking baby food on-the-go, organizing meals, serving meals, and storing ground cereal flours. Glass storage bowls work well because you can see what is inside of them, and glass is a perfectly food-safe material. In addition, tempered glass storage bowls (manufactured by companies like Pyrex or Anchor Hocking) are oven safe, freezer safe, dishwasher safe, and microwave safe. Stainless steel storage containers are also a good food-safe option. Stainless steel containers are typically lighter weight than glass containers, making this type more ideal for taking food on-the-go. Have at least three (1- to 2-cup-capacity) storage containers on hand for thawing puree cubes in the refrigerator. In addition, each "dry-grind" whole food in your menu (grains, lentils, split peas) will require two (1- to 2-cup-capacity) containers for storage (one for the flour and one for the prepared cereal).

TIMER: Used during preparation of purees.

TRASH BOWL: Used for containing scraps from cutting, peeling, and pitting whole foods, limiting trips walking to the trash can or compost pail.

VEGETABLE PEELER: Used for peeling skins off of whole foods.

WATER CONTAINER: When solid foods are introduced, baby should also be introduced to drinking water. Consider purchasing a liner-free stainless steel container to forgo the worry about BPAs and other plastic chemicals. Stainless steel water containers are more expensive than plastic sippy cups, but they last a lot longer. My oldest son has used the same stainless steel water container for more than seven years.

Measurement Conversion Charts

VOLUME

US	IMPERIAL	METRIC
1 tablespoon	½ fl oz	15 ml
2 tablespoons	1 fl oz	30 ml
¼ cup	2 fl oz	60 ml
⅓ cup	3 fl oz	90 ml
½ cup	4 fl oz	120 ml
⅔ cup	5 fl oz (¼ pint)	150 ml
¾ cup	6 fl oz	180 ml
1 cup	8 fl oz (⅓ pint)	240 ml
1¼ cups	10 fl oz (½ pint)	300 ml
2 cups (1 pint)	16 fl oz (⅔ pint)	480 ml
2½ cups	20 fl oz (1 pint)	600 ml
1 quart	32 fl oz (1⅔ pints)	1 L

TEMPERATURE

FAHRENHEIT	CELSIUS/GAS MARK
250°F	120°C/gas mark ½
275°F	135°C/gas mark 1
300°F	150°C/gas mark 2
325°F	160°C/gas mark 3
350°F	180°C or 175°C/gas mark 4
375°F	190°C/gas mark 5
400°F	200°C/gas mark 6
425°F	220°C/gas mark 7
450°F	230°C/gas mark 8
475°F	245°C/gas mark 9
500°F	260°C

LENGTH

US	METRIC
¼ inch	6 mm
½ inch	1.25 cm
¾ inch	2 cm
1 inch	2.5 cm
6 inches (½ foot)	15 cm
12 inches (1 foot)	30 cm

WEIGHT

US/IMPERIAL	METRIC
½ oz	15 g
1 oz	30 g
2 oz	60 g
¼ lb	115 g
⅓ lb	150 g
½ lb	225 g
¾ lb	350 g
1 lb	450 g

ROBERT PLACE

ABOUT THE AUTHOR

LISA BARRANGOU, PhD, is a former corporate food scientist. After becoming a mother, she became passionate about making homemade baby food. She founded the Green Baby Chef, offering personal chef services for infants, and turned her efficient baby food–making strategy into this book, *The Amazing Make-Ahead Baby Food Book.*

Dr. Barrangou is a food enthusiast and food educator who passionately encourages healthy living through eating a diet of predominantly unprocessed whole foods. She holds a BS in nutrition, food, and agriculture from Cornell University, and an MS and a PhD in food science from North Carolina State University. She lives in Raleigh, North Carolina, with her husband, Rodolphe, and three children, Benjamin, Emilie, and Patrick. Visit her website at www.AmazingBabyFood.com.

ACKNOWLEDGMENTS

Watching your own passion and unique vision come to life is a beautiful experience. I am so grateful for the supportive and talented people who took part in this journey with me and helped this book come to life.

To my agent, Marilyn Allen, thank you for finding me, investing your energy, and nailing down the best house possible to publish this book. I'm still pinching myself. To my editor at Ten Speed Press, Lisa Westmoreland, thank you for your guidance, patience, and unwavering support to make sure my voice was clearly heard every step of the way. To the creative team who brilliantly pulled this book visually together—designer Margaux Keres, creative director Emma Campion, and photographer Erin Scott—I couldn't be more pleased. And to my publicist, Erin Welke, my gratitude for your diligent effort in getting this book on the radar and into the hands of more people than I imagined.

A special thank-you to my many recipe tasters and mommy friends. Your feedback has been invaluable. To my dear friend Loan Rathgeber, I will always have immense gratitude for your photography, which initially revealed the true beauty of my baby food recipes and let me see this book would be something special.

Last but not least, my grandest thanks go to my husband and children, the loves of my life and the inspiration for all that I do. Thank you for your patience and support as I worked tirelessly on this project. I'm glad you agree it was worth it.

INDEX